THE INSANITY WITHIN

THE INSANITY WITHIN

P. WALTERS

iUniverse, Inc.
Bloomington

The Insanity Within

iUniverse books may be ordered through booksellers or by contacting:

iUniverse
1663 Liberty Drive
Bloomington, IN 47403
www.iuniverse.com
1-800-Authors (1-800-288-4677)

ISBN: 978-1-4620-7178-4 (sc)
ISBN: 978-1-4620-7180-7 (hc)
ISBN: 978-1-4620-7179-1 (ebk)

Printed in the United States of America

iUniverse rev. date: 12/14/2011

Dedication

For God who gave me the words and wisdom, my husband and
family who supported me, and my dearest friend, Co who read each
chapter as it was being created.

Chapter 1

Bell always knew something was wrong with her mental state but she just couldn't quite put her finger on it. As a child she lived with an alcoholic mother and a father who worked all the time. Finally, at age six Bell's father took her and her sister away from their mother and moved them in with their grandmother who lived in another state. Although their father was a kind man his job demanded long hours out of town and kept him away most of the time. This resulted in their grandmother becoming the primary caregiver. Little did anyone know, the grandmother suffered greatly from mental illness, therefore leaving Bell and her sister to take care of themselves.

The siblings did not get along well together. Bell was overweight and not very attractive, while Dana, Bell's oldest sister, was slim in stature and extremely beautiful. Dana loved all kinds of animals and would routinely drag a lost kitten or puppy home. Bell couldn't stand it. In fact, the first kitten that Dana brought home mysteriously was found cut up in pieces in the back yard. The puppy had what appeared to be bald patches where someone or something pulled out hair by the handfuls. No one could figure out what was happening to these poor animals. Dana finally noticed Bell's behavior while they were walking in the woods one day. It was a hot, humid afternoon in July. Bell and Dana were walking along trails in the woods behind their grandmother's house. They came upon a turtle. Bell kicked it on its back and placed a heavy stone on top so it couldn't roll over. "What are you doing?" demanded Dana. "Don't you know it will die"? She asked.

"Of course," replied Bell "that's why I did it". She smiled slightly enjoying her sister's horrified look. The darkness deep inside was satisfying and seemed to make her tingle all over. Bell would learn to embrace it and allow it to grow.

"You're sick!" exclaimed Dana as she rescued the turtle and release it into a thicket. "What is wrong with you?" she screamed at Bell. Dana wanted to vomit at the thought of this poor helpless creature being tormented. "It wasn't right," thought Dana, "treating one of God's creatures like that." Leaving Bell in the woods, she wanted to get as far away from her twisted sister as possible.

Something changed between the two girls after that day. Bell started going on walks alone and withdrawing from her relationship with her sister. She began talking to herself and even had an imaginary friend in whom she confided everything. At the time, Bell was twelve years old and although she looked like a twelve year old child, at times she acted more like a five year old, playing dress up, drawing childlike pictures and daydreaming about a prince that would someday ride up on a white horse and sweep her off her feet. Bell, being overweight, had a very low self esteem. She got to where she didn't want to bath routinely and would put up her hair in a ponytail so she wouldn't have to brush it. Her clothing of choice was sweat pants and a ragged t-shirt. It wasn't just her appearance that made people avoid her; it was her demeanor and the weird things she did.

Dana tried to help Bell feel better about herself. She gave her sister a "makeover" and curled her hair to make her feel pretty. She allowed Bell to wear her clothes and even invited some of her friends over to get to know her sister. Bell loved the attention; in fact, she couldn't get enough of it. This desire would last her a lifetime. The problem was that this attention did not last long. One night of hearing Bell tell about all her problems and how no one loved her were enough for Dana as well as her friends. No matter how they tried to raise Bell's spirits, she insisted life was hard and everyone was against her. So things went back to normal around the house, Dana doing her own thing and Bell wandering around in the woods alone.

Bell became increasingly angry. She did everything in her power to get her sister to give her special attention to no avail. Then one day when she was in a particularly self pitying mood, she went to the extreme. She had put a lot of thought into this day. Calling Dana down to the kitchen, she told her sister that she wanted to mend their relationship. She filled a pot full of water and put it on the stove to boil. "Want some hot tea, Dana?" Bell asked sweetly, "We can have a tea party, just you and me, like we used to."

Dana, feeling guilty about ignoring Bell over the past few months complied. As she sat at the kitchen table Bell removed two cups from the cabinets and placed a tea bag in each cup. "Oh, this is going to be so much fun," stated Bell, "just like old times." She sat a cup in front of Dana. She placed cookies on her grandmother's fancy plate and placed them on the table. She had spread their finest china dishes on the table and neatly folded the white linen napkins. Bell gingerly removed the pot full of boiling water from the stove and quickly poured it over Dana's head.

A shrill scream came out of Dana as her skin slowly sloughed off her face. Dana fell to the floor in agony gasping as the boiling liquid penetrated her body. The odor of burning flesh permeated the air. "Oops, I'm sorry", said Bell in a monotone voice. Bell slowly walked to the phone and dialed 911. She took a minute to muster up some tears and cried into the phone. "I accidently spilled hot water on my sister!" She screamed, "Hurry!" Bell stood over her sister until she heard the sirens getting closer to their house. When the paramedics arrived they found Dana on the floor severely burned and not breathing. All of their resuscitative efforts failed. Dana was dead.

Their father never recovered from the loss of his daughter. The story he was told by Bell was certainly not the way the incident happened. Dana, his firstborn beloved daughter was gone. He began to drink heavily staying away from home most of the time. He knew something wasn't right about the story Bell told himself and the Paramedics. Bell seemed too calm about the situation. How could this have happened? He knew the girls were not getting along but what siblings do at that age? Finally, he sank too far into depression to question any further. Now all that was left was Bell and her dysfunctional grandmother.

Bell's grandmother was getting old and some say dementia had set in. Every night she would take a handful of pills, lock the door to her bedroom and go to sleep. It really didn't matter anyhow. It's not like her grandmother had taken an interest in the children so Bell pretty much did as she pleased. Bell would occasionally clean but lately she didn't even bother to do that. Why should she? It was not her place to be the maid. It was enough that she had to check in on her grandmother to make sure she was still breathing. Bell had a couple of friends that she spoke with on the phone or she would just sit on the porch and daydream. This had become her favorite pastime aside from torturing any animal that came within reach which was indeed her favorite of all.

One spring, a baby bird had fallen out of its nest. Bell happened up on it. A tiny blue jay that barely had feathers was hopping around and chirping for its mother. Bell picked up the bird. She stared at the helpless creature for awhile taking in all of its little blue fluffy feathers and its bobbing head that seemed too big for its body. She removed the ribbon from her ponytail and tied the little birds feet together. She moved to a nearby fire ant mound and gingerly stuck her foot in the mound so the ants would swarm. She then threw the helpless little bird atop the mound watching as the ants swarmed for the kill using their violent venomous stings. The baby bird squirmed for about fifteen minutes before it took its last breath. Bell felt empowered as the darkness engulfed her and she loved the feeling. It appeared she had no conscious whatsoever. She didn't feel this when she murdered her sister, maybe because her sister had died so quickly.

There was uneasiness in the air. Bell sat on the front porch swinging her feet back and forth when she decided to form a plan for her life. She certainly didn't want to work for a living but she needed money, and lots of it. She had been taking care of her grandmother whom had become quite ill and bedridden. Her grandmother drew quite the social security check along with a retirement check that Bell cashed every month. She could sign her grandmother's name better that the old woman herself. She paid what few bills they had and then stashed the remainder of the money under the floorboard of her bedroom. All she really had to buy for her grandmother was soup and crackers. She wasn't about to spend good money on groceries. That would mean Bell would actually have to cook for the woman and then clean up afterward. Bell would walk down to the local diner and have her meals. Bell pondered what she could do to make a living . . . then it hit her. She could take care of elderly people and they would be so grateful that they would leave her their money. She had to play it right, though, because she had to convince them she was their friend and caretaker. "This will be a piece of cake" she thought.

She knew her grandmother had a large life insurance policy and had named Bell as the beneficiary. She decided it was time to leave the confinement of a sick, elderly old woman and go out on her own. She had just fed her grandmother soup laced with just a pinch of arsenic. Sick as her grandmother already was she just needed a little something to ensure the old woman would not live throughout the week. Her grandmother began to have violent seizures and at times stopped breathing for a few minutes. Bell watched these episodes with great interest. Her grandmother's eyes would roll back in her head and bloody foam would ooze from her mouth. After the second convulsion Bell's grandmother turned to her and begged her for help. "I love you, Bell! Please help me!" she whispered. Bell turned her head as if she never heard a word. All of sudden there was no movement from the bed. Her grandmother had uttered her last words. Bell decided it was a good time to take a walk in the woods.

After returning home Bell called 911 and told them she believed her grandmother had passed away. Bell sobbed as the paramedics wheeled her grandmother out of the house. Since the old woman had been ill for years there was no need to question her demise. Bell's grandmother died of "complications from extensive illnesses" according to the death certificate. Although Bell had saved a great amount of cash there was no funeral and her grandmother was buried in an unmarked grave in the county cemetery.

Bell felt elated. She now owned her grandmother's home and had plenty of money from the life insurance policies as well as all the money she had scammed from her grandmother over the past few years. "Wow!" Bell thought, "Making money is easier than I thought". She decided to go to the library and check out some books. She searched the shelves and found books titled "Making Their Money Your Money" and "How Caretakers Take All". Bell studied them everyday memorizing the steps and legalities of caretakers. She poured over the books day and night planning her future of wealth. She found that if she can just get the families of the elderly prospects out of the way she would con them into signing away all of their assets. "This may be difficult but not impossible," she thought. Now all she had to do is pick a victim.

Chapter 2

The day was warm with a gentle western breeze blowing the aromatic wisteria now blooming in the trees. Bell had been feeling depressed and lonely but today she felt better. She had lost some of her weight and had her hair styled professionally. This was the first time she was actually somewhat attractive. She picked her most revealing dress she could find and decided to find companionship. She had met a few men at church but she really needed someone who would not judge her. She didn't want to get too close to anyone for fear they would find out the things she had done. The local bar was open so Bell decided to have a drink. As she entered she saw a couple of men sitting at the bar and four more sitting at tables. "Well" she thought, "Which one looks like he may have some money to spend on me?" Bell sat at the bar and ordered a whiskey sour.

"Hello", a voice said, "Is anyone sitting here"? Bell turned to see a very handsome man wearing a polo shirt and blue jeans. It was apparent from his accent that he was not from the local area. "No," Bell replied, "Nice to have company". The man sat down and introduced himself. "My name is Ben." "It's nice to meet you, Ben. I'm Bell." The two of them talked for hours. Bell told Ben her pitiful story about how her father took her away from her mother and then abandoned her, leaving her to take care of her sick grandmother. She really liked the sympathetic attention she was receiving from Ben. He had recently moved to the small, rural town. He hadn't met any of the locals and was lonely for companionship. Bell, feeling slightly woozy from the alcohol, attempted to stand but swayed slightly. "Whoa there," said Ben, "Let me help you. Put your arm around me and lean on me." Bell complied and Ben walked her to his truck. "This isn't my car!" She exclaimed. "I can drive!" Ben gently sat her down is his truck and explained, "I can't have you driving in your condition. I'll drive you home and will pick you up tomorrow to get your car." The two of them proceeded to Bell's house. Ben walked her up the stairs of the porch and bid her goodnight. "I'll pick you up at 10:00 am," he said. "You're sweet. Thank you." She replied. Ben got in his truck and left leaving Bell at her door.

The next morning Bell awoke with a terrific headache. She smiled, remembering the man she met yesterday. Although he appeared quite a bit older than her, she definitely was attracted to him. From what she learned yesterday Ben made good money working for the phone company. He owned two homes and a large boat. He was single and had never been married (So no ex-wife to deal with). This sounded like her kind of man! The phone rang and it was him. "It's 9:00 am and I just wanted to let you know that I'll be there at 10" he said. "Thanks," replied Bell, "I'll see you then. I had a wonderful time yesterday." "Me too," said Ben. They hung up the phone. Ben was oddly attracted to Bell. He thought she was nice and although he wasn't looking for a serious relationship she filled the emptiness in him. He was not a shallow man looking only for pretty women; he had his fill of those who were self centered and selfish.

Ben picked Bell up at 10:00 am and took her to breakfast before picking up her car. They decided to spend the day together. Bell was on her best behavior. Ben was clueless to the deep, dark side of her. She had to be very, very careful that he didn't find out her secrets. They walked in the park, had a picnic lunch, and finished their day out by taking in a movie. She invited him to spend the night.

Ben was a very private person having lived by himself for the last eight years. His parents had moved to England several years ago and although he didn't get to see them very often he spoke with them weekly. He was an only child who knew the meaning of working for a living. His parents were retired school teachers and although made a decent living by no means were wealthy. Ben had been very lonely since his parents' move but found solace in his work. He also liked to read so he would spend hours at home at night reading his favorite novel. Ben believed that Bell was good for him and eased his loneliness. He had no idea about the darkness that dwelled deep inside.

Ben was the first man that Bell had ever been with. It wasn't the pleasant experience that everyone talked about but at least Bell now had a boyfriend. She never had any kind of boyfriend before so this was a new experience for her. By this time in her life Bell has become accustomed to her daily routine. She would get up late in the morning and head to the nursing home to visit with the elderly. Actually she was scoping out a potential victim. She would then go to one of her various support groups at the local churches, and by dinner time she would get a free meal from either the food pantry or one of the church groups that prepared meals for the elderly and poor. Bell had everyone convinced that she was a poor woman who couldn't function because of her mental illness. It was true that Bell indeed had a mental problem but the dire conniving and meanness was not part of the disease. She wallowed in self pity and resented anyone who did well for themselves. She worshiped the almighty dollar more than any person should. She became such a tightwad that she wouldn't even buy herself food or clothes, rather choosing to beg for items from charity groups. She was even seen rummaging in the neighbor's trash for anything usable. This behavior became more prominent as she matured.

Ben opened the door to his apartment after spending the night at Bell's. He walked in to an exceptionally clean environment and headed to the shower. Pondering the previous night, he wondered if Bell had ever been with a man. She seemed very inexperienced and additionally something didn't appear to be quite right. "Maybe I'm just being paranoid about forming a relationship", Ben thought. Bell's not the most attractive girl Ben had been with but she seemed nice enough. She seemed to lack self esteem. Ben was not a person to judge people on appearances, rather chose to get to know them. She was sweet and seemed so innocent and he enjoyed her company. While getting dressed Ben decided to give her a call and see if she wanted to go out again tonight.

They saw each other almost every day and would spend the weekends together. Bell seemed to be the perfect girlfriend. She was very attentive to Ben and appeared to care for him deeply. He knew he didn't love Bell but it was nice to have someone to be with. He had been so lonely and she was nice to him. She seemed to be a loving, Christian woman who he could talk to and share his feelings. He never saw the dark side of her. They took long walks in the park after attending church services and would spend many hours just holding hands and watching the sun set.

They had been dating for about six months when Bell decided he was the one for her. She had made up her mind that she was going to convince Ben to marry her. She would ask him tonight.

He picked her up to go out to dinner. During the latter part of dinner Bell brought up the subject of marriage. Ben had drunk quite a bit of wine and Bell had slipped a little something in his drink. (This should ensure that at least he wouldn't blow up and leave.) She told him that she loved him and wanted to spend the rest of her life with him. She knew he cared for her but wasn't quite sure how much. Bell explained that it was foolish for them to live apart when they spent every spare moment together. She told him that their life would be complete and they would no longer be lonely as long as they were together.

"We could get married tonight!" she exclaimed, "I have my cousin who is a pastor at my church ready to marry us!"

"I don't know," Ben replied, "This is a big step for me. I care for you deeply, Bell, but I don't know if I'm ready to get married."

"Please?" Bell begged, "We've been dating for months. We're practically living together now so it's just a formality."

By this time the drug Bell had put in his drink was taking effect. Ben couldn't think straight and the drug was making him compliant. "Whatever makes you happy, Bell" he replied.

She quickly requested the check and asked for Ben's credit card so she could pay for their meal. They walked to Bell's car as she dialed her cousin's phone number.

"Hello," Pastor Rich answered.

"Hey, this is Bell. He said yes!" she exclaimed.

Pastor Rich had only heard Bell's view on the upcoming nuptials. Bell not only attended his church but she was a distant cousin on his mother's side of the family. As far as he was concerned Bell was a little strange but seemed genuinely in love so he had agreed several weeks ago to marry them. Pastor Rich was not aware of the things Bell had done. She was very careful to appear to be a Christian around the people of the church. She had told everyone all about Ben and how he was so in love with her.

"Bell, are you sure you don't want to plan a small ceremony at the church and invited your friends and family?" asked Pastor Rich

"No! No! "She exclaimed loudly. "We want to be married tonight!"

"Ok, Bell. I'll be ready when you get here", he replied.

As Bell and Ben pulled into the driveway of the parsonage of the church, Ben felt a little strange in the head. It was like he knew what was going on but had no control over it. He had never felt this way before and he didn't like it at all. He was conscious enough to know what was going on but didn't appear to be able to control the situation.

"Bell," he said "I don't feel well at all. Maybe we just need to go home until I can get over this"

Bell wouldn't hear of it. "If you really cared for me like you say, then you will do this." She said, "If you don't marry me TODAY then I don't want to ever see you again!"

Ben couldn't think straight. The drug had made him have no control whatsoever. He just didn't want any confrontation at all so he complied. Bell and Ben officially became husband and wife. Everyone in the neighborhood was amazed that Ben actually married Bell including Bell's distant family members. She was such a strange person and he seemed so normal.

Chapter 3

Ben decided to take a job on the oil rigs in the Gulf of Mexico. Bell had been badgering him to make more money so he thought this was a good idea, especially since things had been strained lately. They had been married less than three months when Bell decided she needed more money. She told Ben she was unable to work because of back problems and encouraged him to work extra. Ben did it only because he did not like arguing with her. When Ben got the opportunity to work on the oil rigs, not once did Bella say anything about how she was going to miss him or how she may be worried about him working out on the ocean . . . nothing. All she said was "Make sure your checks are direct deposited so I can have access to them."

Ben assured her that he had taken care of everything as he packed for his new job. He would be gone for sixty days then home for two weeks then gone again. Bell was looking forward to Ben's leaving. She didn't have to continue this act while he was gone. She could finally be herself for two months at a time! Bell rejoiced inside while watching Ben pack. "Poor Ben," she thought, "he really thinks I give a damn if he's home or not." It was obvious that Ben was going to miss home more than anyone at home was going to miss him.

"Just lock the door when you leave," she said, and left the room to take a nap.

Ben just looked at the doorway in disbelief. "I can't believe she didn't even stay awake long enough for me to leave," he thought. The disappointment soon turned to anger. Ben left without a single goodbye spoken. This turned into their routine for the next few years.

She woke up early the next day with big plans. She met a wealthy, elderly gentleman at the nursing home where she volunteered. It seemed he had taken a shine to Bell. He told her she was a sweet young lady who reminded him of his own daughter. Bell could certainly put on an act of kindness when she had a mind to. She stopped at the local bakery to pick up some pastries then headed to the home. Mr. Polk was lying in bed, pale and cold to the touch. "The old man is dying," Bell though, "I have to work quickly. She sat down on the bed beside him and kissed him on the forehead.

"Bell, is that you?" he softly asked.

"Yes, it's me", she replied, "Are you alright?"

"Yes, dear, it's just a little bout with my bronchitis. The doctor came last night and gave me a shot and some medicine to take. He said I should be much better in a couple of days".

"Well, I certainly don't see your children here to help you. Let me take care of you", stated Bell as she fluffed his pillow. "I care about you even if your kids don't". Bell had just planted the seed of doubt in the old man's head. She stayed with him all day and returned day after day until he recovered.

"You are so good to me, Bell. If I can ever do anything for you please let me know", stated Mr. Polk. Those words were burned into Bell's brain. "On, I think you'll be doing quite a bit for me", she thought.

Mr. Polk was a kindly old man who made his fortune in the retail business. He had owned several clothing stores throughout the state. When he retired he sold off all his businesses and stashed quite a savings. He was very lonely as his children lived in another state and rarely saw them. He was flattered that this young woman gave him so much attention and didn't understand why she befriended him but was certainly glad she did. She seemed like a part of his family.

Bell convinced the old man that he would be much better off if he lived at home and allowed her to stop by daily to check in on him and take care of him. Mr. Polk had always been self sufficient until he became sick and he certainly did not want to be in a nursing home. This was a dream come true for him. Since he appeared sharp mentally, he signed the papers to allow Bell to take him out of the nursing home and drive him to his residence. "How lucky I am," thought the old man, "I have someone who cares about me living on the same street." Mr. Polk believed that Bell was sent to him by God.

Bell came by daily to visit the old man, cooking his meals, cleaning, and spending hours talking to him. She had finally convinced him that his children didn't have time to come by and really didn't care about him. Mr. Polk was adamant that Bell was the only one in the world that truly cared. Her plan was working out just fine. After several months, the old man trusted Bell unconditionally. She gained full access of all of his financial accounts, paying his bills, making deposits, and even cashing his checks. During these months Mr. Polk's mind started to deteriorate and he became more and more dependent on Bell and less aware of his financial state.

Bell started skimming a few hundred dollars at a time from the old man depositing the cash in her safe deposit box at the bank. Whenever Mr. Polk asked about his money, she would show him documents that she created to look like official bank statements. This would satisfy him. She took money wherever she could without sending up a red flag to the banks. Mr. Polk's life savings was gone in approximately twelve months. He signed over the deeds to all of his properties as well as changed his life insurance naming Bell as the sole beneficiary and gave her his Power of Attorney. She promptly cashed out all of his investments and placed the money in her safe deposit box. When his family came to visit Bell would drug the old man so that he didn't even know who they were. Bell convinced them that he suffered from dementia. She seemed very concerned and believable to the family that they didn't even question what she had to say and appeared grateful that someone so caring was taking care of their loved one. Since Mr. Polk didn't seem to know who they were their visits became fewer and fewer.

Ben would come home in between jobs and was actually very impressed that Bell had assumed a caretaker role. She just didn't initially seem like the type of person that would care for an elderly person since she had complained so much in the past about having to care for her grandmother when she was younger. "Maybe she's just maturing," thought Ben. "After all, she was practically a kid when all that happened." Things were difficult for Ben because he never really quite understood what all had happened the night they got married; never dreaming it could have been something out of his control. All he knew was that he had married this woman and was determined to do the right thing. Although Ben was not madly in love with Bell he did care about her and vowed to do everything in his power to make their relationship work. He believed in the sanctity of marriage even though sometimes Ben wished they had waited to wed.

Ben and Bell's relationship was very unique. Ben would spend a few days at home then leave again for his job. Bell was able to hold things together for those few days, trying to be as nice as possible, all the while thinking that she had to be good if she wanted to continue to get Ben's check and use his credit cards. She had tucked away quite a bit of cash from his checks along with all the money she had scammed from Mr. Polk. "Wow," she thought "I love making money!" Along with the cash Bell also now owned the old man's house. She dreamed of owning all the houses on the block and renting them out. She could be queen of all landlords with money rolling in every month. Bell was not very educated and really didn't realize what it actually took to maintain rental property. In fact her idea of it all was skewed. Nonetheless, that was her dream.

Chapter 4

B en had been gone for two months and was allowed to leave his
job a day early. He wanted to surprise Bell. The surprise was on
him. When he walked into the house the stench hit him. Dirty dishes were
everywhere and it was obvious the cat's litter box had not been changed in
weeks. The smell nauseated him. He stumbled over piles of dirty clothes
as he made his way to their bedroom. Bell was lying in bed with empty
food containers all around her. Prescription pill bottles were everywhere
he looked.

"Bell!" he yelled, "What the hell happened to this place?"

"Stop yelling at me," she cried "I'm sick!"

Now Ben felt like a fool. He didn't understand why Bell wouldn't have
called him if she was so sick that she couldn't take care of herself. "What's
wrong?" he asked "Why didn't you call me?"

Bell sat up in the bed and explained to Ben that she just didn't feel
well and had been seeing her doctor who diagnosed her with depression.
She had been taking her medicine but it really didn't have much effect on
her. She obviously had not bathed in several days and looked like hell.
Her words were slurred and she could not form a complete sentence. A
little bell went off inside Ben's head. Something just wasn't adding up . . .
something was terribly wrong but Ben just couldn't figure out what exactly
it was.

"Ok, let me help you, Bell. First I'm going to the store to get some
food. When I get back I'll starting cleaning up this place. How about you

get a shower while I'm gone and we'll talk later," Stated Ben. He didn't even wait for a response; he just got in his car and headed to the store. His mind was racing. What in the world was going on? How could this have happened since the last time he was home? Who was this woman at his home? All of thoughts flooded his brain as he parked the car and went inside the grocery store.

Ben picked up a few items and headed to the checkout. The cashier smiled at him and announced, "$32.50 please". Ben handed her his debit card.

"I'm sorry", she stated "your card has been declined."

"There's been some mistake," he said, handing her a different card. She promptly swiped his card and said "Thank you. Have a good evening."

Ben gathered his groceries and headed out the door. When he got to his car he promptly called his bank. Luckily his friend Gwen, who worked at his bank, answered the phone and listened intently as Ben explained what had happened. While waiting for his friend to check Ben's mind was racing. What the hell was going on? What's wrong with Bell? Why was his debit card declined? Finally, after what seemed an eternity, Gwen came back on the line.

"Ben, you're not going to like this," she began, "Our records show hundreds of dollars were withdrawn each month from your joint account with Bell. She withdrew cash each week from the ATM machine here at the bank. I'm sorry, but your account is overdrawn by $356.00.

"What about my savings account?" Ben asked as his head was reeling from the news.

"All funds were withdrawn and the savings account is closed," said Gwen, "Bell closed that account two months ago."

Ben had a difficult time speaking as he said thank you and hung up. He sat in his car with his head in his hands for about an hour. What was he going to do? Every dime he had ever worked for and saved was gone. His money left to him by his parents was gone . . . thousands of dollars . . . gone. His shock and disbelief soon turned to anger and rage. What right did that bitch have to take everything away? He had worked like a dog only to find the woman he married had deceived him all these years. Ben started the car and headed home. His chest felt tight and he was sick to his stomach. His knuckles were white as he gripped the steering wheel. His anger was so great he thought about beating the hell out of Bell so he took a few minutes to calm down as his car skidded to a halt in the driveway.

Ben sat in his car for thirty minutes or more pondering what to do next. He finally made his decision as he walked through the front door.

Ben slowly walked into their bedroom and headed straight for the closet. He grabbed his suitcase and started packing. Bella was sobbing uncontrollably while lying on her bed. "I'm leaving you, Bell," he calmly stated. "I can't believe what you've done to me". He continued to pack his belongings.

"I'm pregnant!" she exclaimed, sitting up in the bed, "If you leave me I'll have an abortion!"

Ben froze. This woman is carrying his child and threatening to kill it! For a few seconds Ben thought he was going to faint. He turned to Bell with disbelief.

"What did you just say?" he asked.

"I knew you would leave me so I stopped taking the birth control pills." She said, "I'm serious, Ben, if you leave me I will abort this baby!"

Ben's shoulders slumped as he realized what he had to do. He couldn't allow this woman to murder his unborn child. It was as if his life had been taken from him. He would have to stay with this woman whom he had grown to hate in order to save his child. Ben realized that for the next several years he would be living in hell but would sacrifice these years for his child. Ben agreed to stay.

At Bell's insistence, Ben gladly moved into the spare bedroom. "At least I won't have to share a bed with that witch," he thought. She also insisted that he change jobs when the baby came so he could help her more. Ben worked full-time as a plumber as well as doing security part-time. This made everyone happy—Bell was happy Ben was out of the house making money, and he was glad to be gone.

Other than the trips down the street to see Mr. Polk Bell spent most of her time in bed stating she was "sick". She would smile at the fact that she had power over Ben. Now that a baby was involved she could convince him to do anything. He wouldn't dare do something to jeopardize the opportunity for him to be around his son or daughter. She had it made! When Ben came home on Fridays he would hand Bell his paychecks. This made her very happy.

One day Ben came home and handed her cash after he had cashed his check. "What are you doing cashing your paychecks?" she screamed, "Are you trying to stash money away to leave me?"

"No," Ben quietly replied, "I was hungry and didn't have my debit card so I stopped by the bank so I could eat".

"You're lying," she said accusingly, "You're going to leave me!"

Ben just shook his head and went to his room locking the door behind him. It wasn't worth the argument. By this time Bell was in her eight month of pregnancy and was hateful beyond belief. She didn't clean, bathe, or even leave the house for that matter. She would just lie in the bed and complain. She did however, manage to get her fat ass up in the afternoons and drive down to Mr. Polk's house. Ben didn't understand her loyalty to this old man. Maybe she reminded him of her father or something. Ben didn't give it too much thought, he just didn't care anymore.

The baby was born the following week; a precious little girl they named Bethany. Mother and baby had to stay in the hospital for a couple of days due to slight complications from the delivery. Ben stayed by Bell's side the entire time. That was the right thing to do. He was at Bell's beckon call. He would take care of the baby at feeding time, change her diaper, then rock her to sleep while Bell sleep peacefully from the pain pills.

After arriving home Bell went straight to the bedroom stating she wasn't feeling well leaving Ben to tending the baby. Bell slept all day and into the night. Baby Bethany awoke every two hours for her bottle and diaper change. Ben couldn't remember when he had last slept. Maybe Bell would give him a break with the baby in the morning. He had taken the week off from work but had to return in a few days and he felt like he hadn't slept in a week.

It was the last day Ben had off before returning to work. Bell was up early getting dressed to go out. She had plans to attend a support group for her mental illness and visit with the ladies at her church. She received lots of attention at these meetings and enjoyed being the center of attention. She would tell the group of how her husband is no longer interested in her and what a difficult time she was having with the new baby. She made it sound like she had to care for Bethany all by herself with no help from Ben. She told the group she had been sick and didn't know how she was going to make it with a new baby. The men and women in the support group all gathered around Bell as she cried, patting her on her back. Bell loved it! She finally found someone who would supply all the sympathy she demanded. Little did the group know that all of this was lies invented by Bell?

"Bell," said Ben, "I need to get some sleep. Aren't you going to take care of Bethany today?"

"No!" she shouted, "You're the one that wanted this baby so take care of her!" Bella stormed out the door

Ben dropped his head. What will happen to the baby while he was working? He would have to talk to Bell about caring for their daughter. He had to work so they could live so he would speak with her when she came home.

Bell came home late in the afternoon complaining of a headache. She tried to go to bed but Ben was adamant about "the talk". He explained to Bell that is was impossible to stay up all night, every night and work during the day. He told her if she would just help out during the day he would sleep when he got home in the evenings and take care of Bethany at night. Bell agreed, after all she needed Ben to bring home a paycheck every week. Additionally, the baby could sleep most of the day and be up when it was Ben's turn to babysit.

For the following couple of weeks the schedule seemed to work out okay. Bell would put the baby in bed with her in the morning when Ben left for work. She managed to care for the infant during the day but at nine o'clock she handed the baby to Ben and went to bed. Ben noticed a severe diaper rash on the baby; redness and sores covered her bottom. Ben carefully spread the ointment on her as she screamed in pain. Having run out of diapers he went to the closet to look for more. There he saw a pile of used diapers that had been wet and obviously had been laid out to dry then stacked in the closet. The smell of urine was overwhelming. "What the hell?" thought Ben?

Ben went into Bell's bedroom. "Bell, what are all of the diapers stacked in the closet?" he asked, "They look like they've been used and dried."

"They were just wet", replied Bell "I laid them on the porch to dry. There's no need in just wasting them." Bell rolled over with her stomach and pulled the covers over her head.

"Do you not even have two brain cells to rub together?" he bellowed, "That baby has a terrible rash! Those are disposable diapers, Bell; you can't dry urine soaked diapers and plan on reusing them!" Ben was flabbergasted with disbelief at the stupidity of this woman. Who in their right mind would do something like this?

He slammed the bedroom door. Luckily he had another box of diapers in the car. "What a nut case!" he thought. Ben fed and changed the baby then gently laid her in her crib after she fell asleep. Ben went to the closet and filled a trash bag full of the used diapers. What normal human being would even think to reuse disposable diapers? At that moment Ben made a promise to himself. If he could just stay long enough to until Bethany could at least become able to feed herself, he was leaving. He couldn't take it anymore.

On Bethany's third birthday Ben came home early from work. They had planned to have a small family party for her. He walked in the door and was shocked. His daughter sat in the middle of the kitchen floor covered in flour. She had pulled everything out of the lower cabinets and had opened every box and bag she found. Sugar was poured all over the floor along with spices, cornmeal and anything else her little hands could open. She smiled when she saw her father and stated proudly, "Look, Daddy, I cook!" Ben couldn't be mad at her; she was only three years old. But where was Bell? She was supposed to be watching her! Ben headed to the bedroom door. He was so angry at his incompetent wife that he could feel his face becoming flushed.

"Bell!" He shouted, "Where are you?"

He stopped in his tracks when he saw Bell just getting up out of bed, She obviously had been asleep for quite some time since she had the imprint of her pillow on the side of her face and the fact that Bethany had opened so much stuff in the kitchen.

"Get your ass out of bed! Our daughter has been left alone and could have gotten hurt while your fat ass is laying up here in bed! Get up!" Ben screamed. He promptly turned on his heel and left the room. He gingerly picked up Bethany and headed to the bathroom to give her a bath. He dressed her in one of her pretty dresses that he had bought for her birthday and brushed her long, curly hair. She looked up at Ben and smiled. Bell still hadn't come out of the bedroom so he and Bethany jumped in the car and went to town to celebrate. Ben hadn't even bothered to try to clean the kitchen. He would worry about that later. Right now he and his daughter would celebrate her birthday . . . without Bell.

Bell had heard the door slam so she slowly crawled out of bed. "Thank God they're gone," she thought. She stumbled into the kitchen to assess the mess Bethany had made. The pills Bell had taken were starting to wear off. "I need more medicine," Bell said aloud but she decided if she didn't want to hear Ben moan and complain she probably needed to clean up the kitchen.

When Ben and Bethany returned Bell had attempted to clean the kitchen. She was actually awake and had bathed. She was very sorrowful for her recent behavior and apologized to Ben over and over. In order to have a somewhat normal evening he accepted her apology. Bethany was quietly playing with her toys while Ben and Bell settled in for a quiet evening. Ben had bought dinner so all they had to do is sit back and relax. Bell seemed more like her old self. She made pleasant conversation and was trying hard to please Ben. She made drinks and snacks while they watched a movie. Bethany was worn out from the birthday events so she went to bed early. Ben fell asleep on the couch during the movie so Bell covered him with a blanket and softly said "goodnight".

The next morning Ben awakened with a start. Bethany was standing beside him crying. "Mommy yelled at me", she bellowed. Ben still couldn't quite wake up. It was like someone had slipped him something in his drink last night. He felt groggy and lightheaded. He picked up his little girl to comfort her when he heard Bell yelling. Bethany clung to his shoulder in fear.

"Bell," he yelled into the bedroom, "What's going on?"

"Our child is dumb as a rock! "She exclaimed, "All I asked her to do is to let me sleep and she looks at me like I'm an idiot! She comes in my room, wakes me up by jumping on the bed then runs out here when I tell her to stop. I don't feel well and nobody here gives a damn!"

Chapter 5

Ben knew it was going to be one of those days. Since it was a beautiful Sunday morning he decided to take Bethany to the park so they didn't have to hear Bell complain all day. His didn't know how much more he could take but he knew he had to bide his time to get away from this marriage. Ben felt guilty in the happiness he felt just thinking about leaving Bell. He would also be leaving his child; no court in the state would grant him custody. If he could just get away maybe he could save his daughter from the crazy and bizarre woman. Someday soon . . .

Ben and Bethany walked slowly to the park. The spring flowers were blooming and the air was warm and inviting. Bethany skipped all the way there then took off running when she saw the slides. She immediately crawled up the ladder and squealed with delight as she slid down only to do it all over again. Ben sat on the bench nearby and watched as the children played.

There was one particular little boy who seemed to be enjoying himself as the woman with him walked gracefully toward Ben and sat next to him on the bench. She smiled and said, "Hello".

"Hi," Ben replied and smiled. "Is he yours?" he said as he pointed to the little boy with freckles across his face and the remains of ice cream on his shirt.

"Yes," she said, my name's Annette and that's Hunter"

"Mine's Ben and that's Bethany", he stated pointing to his little girl. "What a beautiful day!"

"Yes," she agreed, "it certainly is".

Annette was a very striking woman. She had jet black shoulder length hair with crystal blue eyes. Her smile was instantaneous with little dimples on each side of her mouth. She was thin in stature and seemed quite confident with every movement of her tanned body. Ben couldn't help staring and was almost speechless whenever she looked his way. The kids where playing quietly in the sandbox and seemed to getting along great. He thought how wonderful it would be to be with someone like her. She wasn't wearing a wedding ring and he wondered if she was married. Suddenly Ben had a wave of guilt. How stupid to even think something like that! He was a married man with a small child. Although he really didn't have any type normal relationship with his wife the fact was that he indeed was married and sincerely believed in the sanctity of marriage no matter how bad it was. Still . . . it wouldn't hurt to dream a little.

They both heard the scream when Hunter fell and hit his head. Although there appeared to be a lot of blood the wound was superficial. Annette picked up her son and quickly stated, "It was very nice to meet you Ben. Maybe we'll see each other again." She then turned her attention to the sobbing little boy and they slowly walked to their car.

It was getting late so Ben called for Bethany to go home. Home . . . not really a home, just a house that he had grown to hate because of Bell. He could deal with crazy but despised dealing with her meanness. He kept telling himself that in a few more years he could leave. For the second time today a wave of guilt spread over Ben. He would have to leave Bethany, his sweet wonderful child; however he had come to realize that he couldn't help his daughter if he continued to live there. Someday he would find happiness again, but not today.

Annette comforted her little boy in the car and cleaned his wound, just a small cut above his eye. He would be fine, she assured him. Finally, his sobbing stopped and he grinned at his mother amidst his tearstained, dirty face. "I love you mommy!"

"I love you too sweetie," she replied. Annette took him for ice cream before heading home.

Annette was a nurse at a local trauma hospital. She too was married but had lived a horrible life with her husband who drank too much along with his various drug habits. She, like Ben, dreaded going home. She was sure that tonight would be another argument as had been the norm for several months. Sure enough, when she arrived home her husband was highly intoxicated and cursing.

"Where the hell have you been?" he screamed.

"I took Hunter to the park," she quietly replied.

"It's all about Hunter, isn't it? You haven't cooked anything for dinner and my clothes are still in the dryer. You know I'm going out tonight." He glared at Annette as she set her stuff on the kitchen table. She could tell by his actions that not only was he drunk but obviously was high on something else. She was sick of arguing everyday with this man and had grown to hate him. Just hearing his voice made her want to choke.

Tyson, her husband, had been going out every Friday night for the past eight months only to return on Sundays. She couldn't wait for him to leave. She promptly heated the clothes in the dryer and handed them to him. He snatched his clothes and headed to the bathroom to change and get ready for his night out. Annette took Hunter to his room to play until Tyson left. Only when she heard him slam the door and start his car did they dare venture out into the living room. "Finally!" she thought, "Peace at last." She gave Hunter a soothing bath and they both settled in on the sofa to watch a movie. Shortly after Hunter fell sound asleep. Annette's mind began to wonder about the man she had met in the park . . . Ben. He seemed so nice and what a gorgeous man! "I wonder what it's like to have a husband like that," she thought. She had always believed that couples should stay married for the children's sake no matter how bad the relationship. Annette began to softly cry. "There's got to be a better life out there other than the one that I'm living now," she thought. She realized that she couldn't continue to expose her little boy to the wrath of his father and she no longer wanted to be married to this man. A decision was made.

Tyson came home late Sunday night after everyone was asleep. Annette had moved into Hunter's room several months ago so he didn't awaken her when he fell onto the bed in a drunken stupor. He got up early on Monday morning and left before Annette woke up.

Annette heard his truck start up and was relieved when she heard him pull out of the driveway. She immediately got herself and Hunter dressed to go into town. She had an agenda. Annette went to the local attorney's office to file for divorce. She had repeatedly asked Tyson to leave but he had refused so she would have to have him removed from their home.

Annette knew she could no longer put up with the unhappiness knowing that life was too short to be so unhappy. Luckily, the attorney was in and would see her. They immediately started divorce proceedings.

When Annette arrived home she had just a few hours before her evening shift at the hospital began. She was starting dinner and her heart sank when she heard her husband's truck in the driveway. Tyson entered the doorway and immediately began apologizing to Annette.

"I'm so sorry. I don't know why I treat you so badly but I really don't mean the things I say to you. Why don't you call in sick and stay home with me tonight?"

"I can't call in sick and you know it," she flatly stated. "Tyson, I'm going to divorce you!"

Tyson smiled as if she had just told him a joke. "You can't divorce me, Annette. You and Hunter would starve to death and how would you pay the bills? No man is going to want you so you'll be all alone. You don't realize it, but you're lucky to have me." He chuckled as he walked away to sit in front of the television for the rest of the night. Annette took Hunter to the babysitter's house and drove to work. She couldn't leave Hunter with his father for fear that Tyson would get high and neglect his son. Tyson was good with it because he could go and do anything he wanted without a kid in tow.

Annette had a particularly hard night at work. She worked in the emergency department. They had so many patients that the waiting room stayed full all night long. She was exhausted as she drove to pick up Hunter and then go home. To her delight Tyson had already left to go to work. He worked at the local warehouse from which Annette had received multiple calls from to inform her of her husband's infidelity. She didn't care. She actually had hoped he would find a woman, fall in love and leave her alone. Finally, she could sit down and doze while Hunter played quietly beside her.

Chapter 6

Ben and Bethany arrived at home only to find Bell in a stupor after having taken so many pills. Ben gave his daughter a bath and put her to bed. Bell was sitting on the couch wearing only a robe that was open in the front showing her nakedness beneath it. She was grossly obese and had not shaved anywhere in months. Ben felt disgusted but refrained from saying anything for fear of starting an argument. He could tell that Bell was in one of her moods so he didn't even speak but went directly to his bedroom to read. He couldn't get the image of the woman he had met in the park out of his head. He didn't feel guilty this time thinking about her. In fact, he was comforted in the thought of her. Ben fell asleep daydreaming of this incredible woman.

The summer was spent with Ben working most of the time and Bell lying in the bed complaining about anything and everything. Thanksgiving was today and Ben was looking forward to a home cooked meal. Bell had promised that she would make turkey with all the fixings. Ben showered and took Bethany outside to play while Bell prepared the meal. At 1:00 Bell called them in to eat. He didn't see anything on the stove and watched in awe as Bell placed slices of turkey from a package on a plate, poured a jar of gravy on top, and stuck it in the microwave. She put the plate in front of Ben and seemed proud that she a just cooked a Thanksgiving meal. Ben couldn't believe it!

"Is this it?" he asked.

"No, I have pumpkin pie in the frig." She said smiling.

26

Ben was so flabbergasted that he just ate the food and kept his mouth shut, thinking "never again!" Ben wasn't a chef but this was the most pitiful Thanksgiving dinner he had ever seen. He had offered to go buy a big meal but Bell had insisted she was cooking and had promised him it would be grand. He finished the food on his plate and promised himself this would be his last Thanksgiving with this crazy woman.

Christmas morning came and Ben was rushing home from work after pulling a midnight shift. He could hardly wait to see his daughter open the presents he had bought. When he opened the door his heart sank. Bell had allowed Bethany to open all her presents before he got home. Bethany had obviously been up for awhile because she was sound asleep on the sofa. Bell met Ben at the door with his present from her in hand. He was speechless as he opened his gift at Bell insistence only to find she had wrapped a pair of his favorite pants that he had been wearing all year. Ben blew up! He didn't care what the gift was just that someone would take the time to buy him something other than stealing his own clothing and wrapping it for a gift. What idiot would do this?

Bell didn't want to hear it. She immediately ordered him to leave.

"Get out!" she screamed. I get everything you have and more! I have all the money, the house and anything else I want!"

"Great!" Ben screamed back at Bell, "I hope you choke on it!"

Ben threw his clothes in a bag and left. Although he was angry and saddened by leaving his daughter he suddenly felt relieved. "I'm free!!" He felt almost giddy with delight. It was Christmas Day and Ben wasn't sure where he would sleep tonight or where he would go now but he still felt great. He had saved a couple of hundred dollars that he kept hidden so at least he wouldn't starve. "Today," Ben thought, "begins my new life." Next week I will file for divorce.

Chapter 7

Almost a year passed. Ben was allowed to see his daughter infrequently and only if he came to Bell's house to sit while she took care of a couple of elderly people she had met while attending one of her "support groups". She had put off signing the divorce papers by threatening to never let Ben see his child again. Ben was working day and night holding down two jobs so he could get back on his feet. He had been staying with a guy he had been friends with for years so his rent wasn't expensive. He had been paying off all the bills that Bell had created in his name and was close to paying off the final one. He could finally see the light at the end of the tunnel.

It was a warm spring day. The fragrance of the wisteria hanging in the trees followed Ben everywhere. He had the day off and was going boating with his buddies from work. Ben was getting his fishing tackle together but didn't notice a piece of glass had broken in the bottom of his tackle box. As he reached in his hand to get a lure the glass deeply cut his index finger.

"Damn!" Ben said aloud. He put pressure on the wound but couldn't get the bleeding to completely stop. The cut was deep into the flesh and all the way to the bone. Ben was not one to seek medical attention but he knew he needed stitches in order for the wound to heal quickly. He called his buddies to go without him and headed to the emergency room.

Ben sat for about a half an hour when he was called back to a room. He sat on the stretcher and waited for someone to come in. Finally, the nurse came in to cleanse the wound. Ben's mouth dropped when he realized the nurse was the woman from the park. It had been over a year but he still remembered her name . . . Annette.

With supplies in hand she turned to Ben. She was astounded! The man she had dreamed of ever since they met over a year ago was sitting in front of her. He was even more handsome than she remembered. She tried to gain her composure but was having a hard time speaking. She dropped the bandaging supplies and just stood there.

"Well hello," piped Ben, hoping she didn't notice how nervous he was.

"Hi," she replied, "long time no see". On my God! That popped out before she realized how stupid it sounded.

Ben smiled from ear to ear. He had dreamed of this woman since the day they met. She was more incredible than he remembered. She still wasn't wearing a wedding ring and he wasn't about to let this opportunity get away. He couldn't be too eager, though, or she would think he was crazy. The doctor arrived in the room and began stitching his wound right away. When he finished, Annette gently placed the bandage and had finally calmed down a little. She explained how to care for his wound and to come back in seven days to have the stitches removed. Ben assured her he would return. They talked for a few minutes making small talk. Since the emergency room was busy Annette had to go. She smiled sweetly at Ben and said she would be here when he returned in seven days.

Ben sat on the stretcher a minute because he just couldn't believe it. He wanted to ask her out but hadn't. Damn! He vowed when he returned he was not leaving until she agreed to go out with him.

Seven days had passed so Ben called the emergency room to make sure Annette was working before he came to get his stitches removed. To his delight she was working there today so he headed to the hospital. When he arrived Annette was actually outside at the picnic tables eating her dinner. She had come in early in order not to miss Ben. He stopped in his tracks when he saw her. Taking a deep breath he tried to slow his pounding heart. There she was . . . what a beautiful woman. It wasn't just Annette's beauty that amazed Ben; she was also a smart, witty, and caring woman. Ben slowly approached her and smiled.

Before he lost his nerve he blurted out, "Annette, would it be too forward of me to ask you out on a date?"

There, he said it. It was out. She probably will refuse but at least he tried. His hands were sweating and he felt faint. His only hope was that she didn't laugh at him.

The pause in the conversation seemed endless. Annette couldn't believe her ears. She never dreamed a man like this would want to take her out on a date. She had dreamed of him for a long time wondering what it would be like to be with someone like Ben. Her self confidence was low regardless how she appeared on the outside. She had tried not to let it show. Her ex-husband had told her how stupid she was and how no one else would ever want to be with her. Deep down she knew better but still had doubts about herself.

"I would love to go out with you," she replied.

"Why couldn't she have said something else? I should have just said yes . . . maybe that would have been too simple? He's probably already wishing he hadn't even asked." She thought.

Ben smiled as they exchanged phone numbers. Annette gave him her address as they planned to go out on Friday. Ben patted her on her shoulder and said, "I'll be there at seven" and walked into the hospital for his appointment thinking the whole time, "God, please don't let my legs give way."

Annette sat for some time afraid that if she tried to stand her legs would buckle. Her heart was racing and it was difficult to breath. She and Ben had a date! Her mind started racing. What was she going to wear? She would have to find a babysitter for Hunter. She would have to think about everything later because she was late getting back to work.

Friday finally arrived. Ben had called everyday during the week and they had talked on the phone for hours on end. Annette knew that he had a crazy ex-wife and young daughter and Ben was aware of Annette's insane ex-husband and young son. What a pair!

Ben arrived promptly at seven as promised. They had decided to go to dinner and a movie. The dinner looked delicious; however Annette couldn't eat much due to the nervous fluttering in her stomach. She couldn't remember when she had been this nervous. Ben was charming and Annette thought he was the most wonderful man she had ever met. They left the restaurant and headed to the movie theater. Ben was quite the gentleman, opening doors for her and holding her hand in the parking lot. They settled in to watch the movie. It was quite scary for Annette so Ben held her hand the whole time. Ben leaned over and whispered, "I'm having a wonderful time," and then without warning he gently kissed her; a soft, gentle kiss that melted her completely. Annette had never dreamed she could feel this way about a man.

Ben's hands were sweating profusely. He had just kissed the woman of his dreams and she seemed to like it. Wow! He could hardly contain himself. He had never felt this way before and was quite uneasy about this new feeling. He had just gotten out of a horrible relationship and certainly wasn't ready to jump into another one but this woman was special.

The movie ended and neither one wanted the night to end. They drove around a little while and decided to go to the local coffee shop. They talked until wee hours of the morning and finally both were so tired they called it a night. Ben drove Annette home, walked her to her door and gave her a long goodnight kiss. "I'll call you tomorrow and again, I had a wonderful time," said Ben.

"Me too," she replied, "Good night, Ben."

Just as he had promised Ben called Annette the next day and again everyday talking for hours. When they both had time off of work they spent their time together. They were falling head over heels in love.

Chapter 8

They had been dating for several months when Annette received a call at work from Bell. The angry woman on the other end of the line was beside herself.

"This is Bell, how long have you been seeing my husband?" Bell demanded.

"To begin with, he is no longer your husband. Secondly, it's none of your business. Do not call me again!" Annette hung up the phone wondering how Ben's crazy ex-wife got her cell phone number. He had warned her about Bell but she had no idea of the things that Bell was capable of doing. Annette knew that at some point Bell was going to find out about their relationship but it was odd that Bell seemed to think that she was still married to Ben. What a weird woman!

Bell hung up the phone, seething with rage. How dare Ben! He was her husband and Bell was not about to let him go. Who was this woman that he's been dating? She was told that Ben and Annette had been dating for months. Would he be so foolish as to marry her? If he thought he could get by with this he'd better think again. Bell vowed to make his life a living hell. She immediately dialed Ben's number. Getting his voicemail, she left him a scathing message.

"This is your wife! If you continue to see this bitch you will not be allowed to see your daughter! You'd better call me back immediately!" Bell screamed into the phone. "I should have killed him when I had the chance," she thought.

Ben listened to the message then deleted it. This crazy woman thinks she's still married! What a nutcase! Ben didn't give it too much thought. Bell has always threatened him but she couldn't touch him now. She couldn't legally keep Bethany from him and he would no longer allow Bell to dictate what he does.

Bell had kept Ben's room like he had never left. He had taken some of his things but she had been telling Bethany that her daddy was working. In fact, she told everyone she knew the same story. Bethany was so young she didn't realize just how long Ben had been gone. Ben no longer would come to their home and babysit his daughter. Although he missed Bethany terribly he was with Annette now and knew it wouldn't be proper for him to spend time at his ex-wife's house even though Bell would leave as soon as he arrived. The more Bell thought about the situation the angrier she became. She devised a plan.

"Bethany!" she called, "you need to take your medicine."

Bethany slowly came in the room. She was used to taking medicine. Bell would take the child from doctor to doctor with multiple complaints. She had even taken her to a psychiatrist at the age of two. Bell claimed that her daughter was "slow" and hadn't developed properly. She said Bethany had a speech problem and was mentally challenged. Since all the information came from Bell the doctors believed her and would prescribe all types of medicines for Bethany. Bell's thought was that if she could get a doctor to diagnose the girl with mental problems then Bell could get a large check from the government for having a retarded child.

Bethany opened her little mouth to swallow the drugs. This time they tasted even worse than before but she gulped them down quickly and drank a soda to get the taste out of her mouth. About thirty minutes later Bethany began to vomit violently. She couldn't stop. Bell smiled as she put her daughter in the car and drove to the hospital. She called Ben on the way to tell him their daughter was very sick and enroute to the emergency room. She had already called the hospital to make sure Annette wasn't working today. Little did Bell know that Ben and Annette were together? Ben assured Bell he was on his way.

When Ben and Annette arrived at the emergency room through the employee entrance the doctors were pumping Bethany's stomach. She had ingested some type of poison. The child didn't look good. She was pale and sweaty and had a tube going in her nose down into her stomach. Her limp little body didn't move as the doctors worked feverishly to save her life. Bell wasn't in the room when Ben and Annette arrived. Since Annette worked there they had allowed the couple to go back to the room. Finally, they had the child stabilized. Bethany opened her eyes, smiled at her daddy and fell asleep. The doctors were very concerned that she had access to a poison so lethal although they admitted they weren't sure exactly what kind of poison she had ingested. After being assured that his daughter would sleep for several hours and that she would make a full recovery Ben decided it was time to leave before Bell found out Annette was with him. Although he desperately wanted to be with Bethany he knew it would only be trouble if they stayed. Annette explained the situation to the doctors before she and Ben slipped out the door.

When Bell was finally allowed in the room and found out Ben and Annette had been there she exploded. She screamed that she had called her husband and he had brought his concubine to the hospital. She was sobbing and yelling so loudly that the staff had to call security to calm her down. "This isn't over!" thought Bell. "How dare they make a fool out of me?"

After a night stay at the hospital Bethany was allowed to go home. Bell had been calling Ben every hour throughout the night but he had obviously turned off his phone. Oh how he would pay for this embarrassment. Did he really think she would allow him to do this to her without paying dearly for it? She drove her daughter home. Her plan hadn't worked and she couldn't believe it! Could Ben really care for this woman? Bell started to cry. She had always believed that Ben would return home . . . she had to think of some way to get him back. Maybe she needed to focus more on Annette . . .

The next day Bell called Annette. "Hello Annette, this Bell, Ben's wife. I'm calling to beg you to let him go. His daughter needs him desperately and he needs to come home with us. We can't survive without him. Please . . . I'm begging you to let him go."

Annette couldn't believe this woman had called her. "Bell, I've asked you not to call me. You need to speak with Ben and not me. If you continue to call my phone I will file a complaint with the police department for harassing phone calls. No don't call again!" Annette promptly hung up the phone.

"That hateful bitch!" thought Bell, "We'll see about that!" She would have to try something different.

Bell had been taking care of a couple of elderly people in the neighborhood and was hoping one of them would die soon. Although she had a large stash of cash in her safety deposit boxes she felt the need for more money. Her support group had been helping her buy things for Bethany but if Ben never returned home her savings wouldn't last forever. She was getting twenty five percent of Ben's paycheck for child support but that too was not enough. She was stealing steady income from Mr. Polk but she wanted more. The little lady she had been taking care of hadn't gotten to the point of fully trusting Bell so it would be a while before she could scam money from her. Bell would only buy clothes for Bethany at the thrift stores and buy groceries at the local dollar store in order to save money. She wasn't spending her money on Bethany that was Ben's job. She had to come up with a new plan. First on the agenda was to find out more about Annette. If she could cause problems between the couple then maybe Ben would realize he belonged at home with his family. Bell began her quest.

Chapter 9

Ben and Annette had been dating for quite some time and Ben decided it was time to pop the question. He loved Annette with all his heart and he was sure she loved him as well. They had planned to go out on Friday night and Ben wanted to make this date special. He had called and made reservations at the Italian restaurant where he would to ask her to marry him. He had it all planned out in his mind. They would have dinner then when desert is served he will get down on one knee and ask her; he knew she would say yes. Ben hadn't intended on getting remarried, in fact, he had given up on the prospect of finding someone he truly loved. He never loved Bell and had regretted time and time again for ever marrying that hateful woman. His mind wandered to Annette. He had never known love until she came into his life; she shared the same values and ethics as Ben. He opened the ring box and stared at the ring that he had bought, hoping she would like it. "It won't be long now," said Ben as he looked at his watch. It was time to get ready and pick up the love of his life.

Annette knew something was up with Ben and she suspected his plan. The couple had talked about marriage for some time and Annette was nervous. She had just gotten out of a horrible marriage and never intended on falling in love. She, like Ben, never really knew true love until now. She adored him and was looking forward to spending the rest of her life with him. Suddenly the door bell rang. It was Ben.

The night went as planned as the two enjoyed a wonderful meal. The waiter brought the desert and Ben promptly fell on one knee and proposed marriage. He was ecstatic when Annette said "yes". This was the beginning of their dreams coming true although neither of them could imagine the problems they both would be dealing with in the upcoming years.

Bell had been forced to allow Ben to see his daughter every other weekend so Ben would pick up Bethany around six on Friday evenings and return her home at six on Sunday. Bell would set Bethany on the front porch to wait for her father. When Ben arrived Bell would scream and curse at him so much that Annette took over transporting Bethany to their home. Bethany was a sweet little girl with blond curls that bounced when she walked. She had crystal blue eyes that seemed to look right through anyone she saw. She adored her father but she did not take kindly to this woman who had suddenly come into her life. Ben used to shower his daughter with gifts and take her to the park to spend the day, just the two of them. Now he always wanted Annette and Hunter to tag along and Bethany did not like it at all. She even told Annette, "I'm here to see my dad and not you." Annette understood that it was hard for Bethany to be away from her dad and tried to make the visits as pleasurable as possible. She would try to make the weekends special but to no avail.

On one particular visit Annette was making wedding plans when Bethany came in the room. "What are you doing?" asked the little girl.

"I'm making plans for my wedding," replied Annette.

"Who ya marrying?"

"Well, your dad of course."

"What? You mean my dad and mom are getting divorced?" asked Bethany as tears welled up in her eyes obviously clueless to the situation between her parents.

"Bethany, your mom and dad has been divorced for years. He hasn't even lived at your house for years. We love you and we were hoping you would consider being our flower girl"

"Momma said he's just been working a lot. He still has his room! You've ruined everything!" screamed Bethany.

"Your mother may be keeping his room Bethany, but your father does not live there. He lives here with me," said Annette, wishing Ben was home to help explain the situation. Bethany stormed off to her room in tears. Annette could not believe that this crazy woman had not told the child that her parents were divorced. Moreover, it was eerie that Bell still kept Ben's room like he had never left. Bethany didn't speak a word when Annette took her home. She just stared out the window.

Bell heard the front door close expecting her daughter to come home. Bethany was crying. She told her mother what Annette had said. Bell was livid. It was bad enough that he was running with this floozy but now she had upset her child. Who did they think they were? Married? Bell was beside herself with rage and didn't try to conceal it from Bethany. She immediately picked up the phone and called Ben. "You ass!" she screamed, "What gives that bitch of yours the right to invite my daughter to your wedding! It's too soon after the divorce! Have you no shame?" Ben didn't want to hear it so he promptly hung up the phone which made Bell even angrier. Bell always believed that Ben would eventually see the error of his ways and return home. Now she began having doubts. She had to break up this relationship.

Bell decided that maybe she could work through Bethany. After the little girl calmed down Bell sat her down on the sofa and begin to fill the child's head with lies. "Bethany, this woman is trying to take your daddy away from us. Your daddy is under her spell so we have to work together to stop her." Bethany, gaining a glimpse of hope listened quietly as her mother continued. Bethany was eight years old now and although she didn't fully understand what was going on she knew she wanted her father home. She would do anything her mother asked.

Bell told Bethany that her daddy didn't love them anymore and it was all because of Annette. Your daddy always wanted a little boy and when he marries Annette he will have one and forget all about you. Bethany listened to her mother intently. Bell explained that if Bethany would misbehave when she was alone with Annette then maybe she would decide not to marry her father. Bethany's little eyes filled with tears. How could her father no longer love her? She just didn't understand. Bell drilled her daughter to the point of brainwashing her. It took a couple of hours but she finally made Bethany understand what needed to be done.

Annette told Ben about what happened between her and Bethany and he said he would speak with her on the next visit. On Bethany's next visit Ben sat her down and explained that he had been gone a long time and how he deserved to be happy. He told her that sometimes parents can no longer happily live together and that people change. Bethany seemed to understand and gave her daddy a hug. Bethany was the ideal child when Ben was around but if he had to work on the weekend of visitation she gave Annette hell. She would tell Annette, "You're not my momma!" and throw a tantrum. Bethany was doing exactly as her mother had coached her. Annette thought that this was just Bethany's way of coping with the divorce of her parents and tried to be understanding. It was hard for Annette as she tried everything in her power to please the child, cooking special treats for her, taking her shopping and going to the movies. As long as Annette was actually doing something for Bethany the girl was nice but if she wasn't catering to her Bethany could very mean and hateful. Bethany resented Hunter who seemed content to play his video games in his room and ignore her demands.

One day Annette took Hunter and Bethany shopping for school clothes. Bethany only wanted the most expensive items and demanded the highest priced shoes in the store. Annette put her foot down and said "no". Bethany threw a fit so much that Annette took them out of the store. Bethany threw her clothes down and stomped on them. Annette's first impulse was to give her a smack on the butt then thought better of it. "We're going home!" stated Annette. They traveled home in silence. When they got home Bethany stormed off to her room and didn't speak to Annette for the rest of the day nor on the way home. Later, Annette found out that Bell had taken the girl's clothes back to the store for a refund, pocketed the money and told Bethany that they were lost. Annette was furious.

Chapter 10

The day of the wedding finally arrived. Bell said it was too soon and did not allow Bethany to be a part of the ceremony. Although Ben and Bell was disappointed they were determined not to let it ruin their wedding. Everything else seemed perfect. The weather was warm with clear skies and sunshine warmed the little chapel that sat among the pine trees. Hunter looked handsome in his tuxedo as he prepared to walk his mother down the aisle. Annette's best friend had planned the wedding. Every little detail had been perfected and the ceremony progressed without a flaw. They were finally married. Ben and Annette were ecstatic. They celebrated late into the night with their friends and family.

Bell was depressed the day of the wedding. She never imagined that Ben would really marry Annette. Her plan to use Bethany to break them up had been too slow. There hadn't been enough time. In her head Ben was still her husband and she would fight for him until her death. Bell had sent Bethany to a friend's house so she could be alone and wallow in self pity. She had thought that if she didn't allow Bethany to attend the wedding they would postpone it which would have given her more time. "How dare he marry that little tramp!" thought Bell. "He belongs to me!" She just couldn't seem to get past the fact that Ben was never coming home. Bell hated Annette with such a passion that sometimes she couldn't even sleep at night thinking about her. Bell had been diagnosed with manic depression and psychosis so the hatred seemed to worsen her condition. "If I could just get rid of Annette I know Ben would come home." She thought with tears flooding her eyes.

The following day Bell set off to visit with the elderly people she had been taking care of. She liked her visits with them because they listened to her tale of woe. Bell told them how her husband had left her for a younger woman and was trying to take her child away from her. They all sympathized with Bell as she told her story. Bell had told the story so much that she actually started to believe that Ben left her for Annette. She would never admit that he left her because she was mean and deceitful and he didn't love her. He really never did, he was just lonesome. When Bell returned home after picking up Bethany she had an idea. She called the local Department of Family and Children's Services and filed a complaint. The complaint stated that Annette had abused Bethany on one of her visits by cursing at her even slapping the child in the face. Even though it never really happed Bell was sure she could convince Bethany to swear to it. The case worker took the report and said they would investigate the complaint. Bell sat Bethany down and drilled into the little girl that Annette really did curse her and hit her and had the child repeat the story over and over until she actually believed it. "If she's going to be married to my husband then she will pay the price!" thought Bell. "I'm going to make her life miserable!"

A knock on the door awakened Annette from her nap. The well dressed lady at the door introduced herself as an investigator with Children's and Family's Services. She was very polite and asked if she could come in. Although Annette had worked all night she smiled and invited the woman to sit. When Annette found out why the lady was there she was astounded. "What?" she asked. "I've never cursed at Bethany and certainly never laid a hand on her." Annette explained the situation with Bell hoping the woman believed her. The investigator's demeanor did not change and stated that because of the possibility of physical abuse the case was being turned over to the local police department. Annette was floored. She couldn't believe her ears. Did Bethany really say that or was Bell making up some bizarre lie in order to cause trouble. Nonetheless, this was a serious allegation and although Annette knew she was innocent she was concerned that they would take Bethany's word over her own. The woman politely explained the procedures and left her card with Annette who immediately called Ben.

Ben was livid. He knew had both Bell and Bethany lied constantly in order to get their way. Now they had accused his bride of striking his child and he would not tolerate it. He had to think quickly in the event the police believed this lie. Ben left work and headed straight to the elementary school where Bethany was having lunch. He checked her out at the front desk and headed to the police department. On the way there he confronted her quite harshly. At first she recited the story she had heard from her mother. When Ben began asking specifics the child caved and start sobbing. She told Ben the truth. Her mother had created the story in order to cause problems. Bethany had been instructed to confirm that Annette had slapped her across the face. Ben was so angry that he had to wait a few minutes in the police parking lot before he and his daughter went inside. Bethany had to calm down as well. She didn't want to accuse Annette of anything but it's what her mother wanted and Bethany wanted to please her mother. She loved her. As they went inside to speak with an officer Ben had a bad feeling that this would not be the only problems they would face concerning Bell.

The officer took the report and said he would forward it to the detective for the possibility that Bell could be charged for false report of a crime. They would also contact the Department of Family and Children's Services. Bethany was so ashamed that she wouldn't even look at her father. Ben returned Bethany to school. She didn't even tell him goodbye; she just jumped out of the car and slammed the door. Now Bethany was the one who was mad. She wasn't sure if she was mad at her mother for insisting she lie or mad at her father for catching her in the lie. Either way Bethany was not happy. She loved her father but she felt betrayed since he married. She also loved her mother very much and felt sorry for the pain that her mother seemed to be going through. The child was torn between her two parents.

Ben arrived home and filled Annette in on the day's happenings. Annette was crushed that Bethany went along with Bell's story. Although Bethany threw her tantrums and said a few unsavory things to Annette she understood that the situation was very hard for the girl. Annette loved Bethany and was really trying to form some type of relationship with her. Ben was disappointed in his daughter. He had raised her to be honest and forthcoming; nothing like the little girl she had become. Bell had really done a number on the child and he despised the crazy, demented woman. Ben apologized to his bride for his daughter's behavior as he didn't know what else to say. He was glad that Annette was understanding and felt sure that police would charge Bell with false report of a crime. Little did they know that Bell had already been contacted by the local authorities and blamed the whole story on Bethany, a confused little girl that was desperately trying to reunite her parents?

Bell was relieved to find the policeman believe her story that Bethany had made up a lie in order to get her parents back together. She was angry at Bethany for breaking down and admitting the truth about the incident because this would surely have splint Annette and Ben. Bell vowed to continue her quest to break up their marriage. She would have to think of something else that didn't involve Bethany since the youngster was weak and wasn't able to stand up to her father. Bell was just trying to get her family reunited.

The next day Bell logged on to the internet and started applying for credit cards in Ben's name. She knew he never checked his credit score and she needed money to help raise his daughter. He may be angry when he found out but he wouldn't send the mother of his child to jail, besides, Bell had committed much more serious crimes in her life than credit card fraud. She was approved instantly for three different cards totaling fewer than thirty thousand dollars worth of credit. Bell was going shopping!

Within a week the credit cards arrived and Bell couldn't wait to get to the mall. She left Bethany with Mr. Polk down the street so she could have a "me" day. She began with getting her hair cut and dyed, then had a manicure and pedicure at the salon, followed by spending the rest of the day shopping for clothes. Bell smiled to herself of the thought that her husband was treating her to a day out. She ended the day by having a very expensive meal before picking up Bethany at Mr. Polk's house. Even though the old man was barely able to get around he had agreed to watch the child. She was no trouble and had spent the day playing video games and watching television. When Bell arrived at his home he told her that he wasn't feeling well and was having chest pain. Bell assured him he was fine and gave him a pain pill. She helped him to his bed and promised to call later to check on him. The old man fell asleep before Bell and Bethany had even made it out the door.

Later that night Bell had fallen asleep on the couch when she was awakened by the sounds of sirens going past her house. They stopped at Mr. Polk's home. Bell stared out the window and watched as a group of paramedics and firefighters surrounded the old man as they wheeled him to the ambulance on a stretcher. Bell went to bed unconcerned that her friend and neighbor had been taken to the hospital. She already had everything she needed from Mr. Polk so she really didn't care what happened to him. She had drained his bank account and his house was signed over to her. She even had his power of attorney. The next morning the hospital called and asked her to come immediately. Bell got dressed and took Bethany to a friend's house explaining she had been called to the hospital. Upon arriving at the emergency room she barged through the doors yelling, "Is he dead yet?" The staff tried to calm her but Bell was on a roll. She had grown tired taking care of the old man. He was always asking Bell to do something for him and she was sick of it. "Is he dead?" she yelled louder. The doctor came out into the waiting room and escorted Bell to the family conference room. He calmly told her that they had been unable to save Mr. Polk. Bell put on a show; she burst into tears and screamed. She was sobbing as the doctor explained that Mr. Polk's heart was just worn out from his diseases and sickness. Bell appeared crushed but in reality she was happy the old man was gone. Now everything he had was hers. She finally calmed and went directly to her attorney's office to get the ball rolling on her fortune. She knew his family would fight her in court but she ensured all the legal papers were in order.

Chapter 11

Annette had taken a few days off to catch up on several things. She and Ben had planned on building a new house. Ben owned several acres of land in the rural part of the county. He had apparently bought this property prior to his divorce but hadn't divulged the purchase to Bell. They were going to build their dream home. Annette pulled her credit report as well as Ben's only to find that Ben was over extended in debt. The report showed several credit cards in Ben's name and a personal loan for ten thousand dollars with a bank in the adjoining state. Ben had never mentioned the cards or the loan. When he arrived home from work Annette confronted him with the report. He was furious. He had no knowledge of the cards or the loan and immediately called the companies that issued them. He found the applications for the cards and loan were made over the internet. They showed the address from his profile as Bell's address. Ben went straight to the police station and filed a report. "Bell is absolutely unbelievable," thought Ben. Annette was so angry that she was in tears. It would be months if and when they rectified this situation. This would delay their dream. She hated Bell.

After several months of phone calls and paperwork mailed back and forth between Ben and the companies, the ordeal was fixed. The credit cards were cancelled and the loan was placed in Bell's name. The police stated that although Bell applied for the credit she had taken responsibility for the loan so they would not press charges. Bell was obviously mentally unstable and the police department wanted no part of arresting someone who would cost them hundreds of dollars in psychiatric evaluations. Actually, the truth was Bell's cousin was married to the police chief. Since it was an election year, he wanted no part of the embarrassment of having a family member so insane. It was quickly covered up within the department and he hoped he could keep it buried at least until after his re-election.

Annette and Ben were beside themselves with anger. When would Bell leave them alone? This was the second time she's broke the law and no one will do anything about her. Ben and Annette normally were very nice and forgiving people but their dealings with Bell had changed them especially when it came to Ben's ex-wife. They had spent several thousand dollars in attorney's fees and were forced to delay building their dream home. Annette didn't seem to take the stress as well as Ben. Maybe it was because he had become calloused to Bell's stupid behavior but Annette just couldn't grasp it. She had never heard of the weird and hateful things Bell had done, not only to her but to Ben and Bethany as well. Annette knew that the doctors at the emergency room had suspected Bell of poisoning Bethany a few years ago but they just didn't have any proof. Annette didn't need any proof; she knew Bell was guilty. The woman deserved to be locked up behind bars for a long time.

Although it needed a lot of repairs Bell rented Mr. Polk's house. She received just a few hundred dollars per month and loved being the "landlord". She rented it cheaply so she wouldn't have to spend money on repairs. The tenants were poor Mexican immigrants so they didn't complain. Bell had liquidated the rest of Mr. Polk's assets and had deposited the cash in her safety deposit boxes. Although she had plenty of money Bell portrayed herself as a poor single mother who had been betrayed by her ex-husband. She continued to go from church to church and eat free meals and shop at the thrift store. The only time she really spent money was when she had received all the credit cards in Ben's name. Now she was responsible for paying off the cards. "Oh well," she thought, "at least I didn't wind up in jail." She would have to be more careful and not let her hatred cause her to make mistakes like that again. It did feel good though, using a credit card with Ben's name on it . . . just like old times. Bell wanted Ben back and she was determined to make it happen one way or the other.

Chapter 12

Annette arrived to pick up Bethany. She never got out of the car but would always honk the horn for Bethany to come out of the house. Annette had been sitting in the driveway for about thirty minutes honking when Bethany finally opened the door. She looked sleepy. "Where have you been? I've been waiting a while for you," stated Annette.

"I was asleep." Bethany replied flatly as she got into the car.

This irritated Annette but she dared not say what was on her mind for fear that the whole weekend would be ruined. Bethany had been complaining to Ben that Annette wasn't treating her fairly when she would come to visit. The fact of the matter was the Bell treated Bethany like a baby. She was eleven years old now and acted like a five year old girl. Bethany still wet the bed at times! Ben insisted it was a reaction to her mother's dysfunction but Annette believed that she wet the bed on purpose. She never had an accident in the middle of the night. It always occurred either just after she went to bed or when she awoke in the morning. Annette, being a nurse, was wise to her little game and would make Bethany change her own linen. This infuriated Bethany who would cry to her father that Annette was "being mean" to her. Ben tried to keep peace so he would go change the sheets and put the wet linen in the wash. It bothered Annette but she didn't want to fight with her husband. Bethany knew just how to act and what to say to make Ben feel sorry for her. He didn't realize that he was doing exactly what the child wanted.

It was Sunday and Bell was getting ready for church. She enjoyed the fellowship with the women there. They would listen to Bell as she told them how her husband had ran off with another woman and how she was left penniless with a small child. They were very sympathetic and offered everything from babysitting services to donations of money. Bell loved it. She loved for people to feel sorry for her and pay her attention. She could break down and cry at will so it was easy to gain sympathy. Today was going to be most enjoyable because the church was having a fellowship day and was serving food. They would always allow Bell to take extra home and she didn't even have to help clean up. Bell would fill up several plates and head home. She and Bethany could eat free for the week.

The next Friday was a beautiful warm day with a gently breeze blowing. Annette waited in the driveway once again to pick up Bethany. The little girl slowly came toward the car hopping on one leg. After she got into the car Annette asked, "What is wrong with your leg?"

"I fell off the porch," she said obviously in pain. The porch was approximately twenty feet high. Annette was perplexed that she wasn't on crutches and didn't understand that if Bethany was hurt why Bell didn't call them.

"Did the doctor say what was wrong?" asked Annette

"I didn't go to the doctor," she replied. "My mom put me in a bathtub full of hot water and then rubbed Ben Gay on my leg. I went to school today and couldn't walk so I've been hopping on one leg. Look at the bruise!"

When Bethany lifted her shorts the child's thigh was completely black and blue. Annette couldn't believe that Bell didn't call an ambulance or at least take the girl to the hospital! "We're going to the hospital right now," Annette exclaimed.

She called Ben on the way to the hospital. They immediately placed Bethany on a stretcher and gave her some pain medication then wheeled her to the x-ray department. The pain medicine was beginning to work when the doctor came into the room. "Annette," he said, "Bethany has suffered a fractured pelvis. It looks like a crack and will probably heal on its own but she has to use crutches for about three weeks."

"Why was this child not seen by a physician?" he asked.

Annette had not divulged much of her personal issues with the people she worked with but quickly explained about Bell. The doctor shook his head in disbelief. "Bethany is very lucky she didn't further damage herself," he stated. "The pelvic ring is fractured and by putting weight on her legs could have severe consequences. The mother should be arrested." He promptly left the room in disgust.

Ben was working out of town so he arrived at the hospital just as Bethany was being released. His daughter was on crutches and seemed to be in quite a bit of pain. Thank God for Annette. He didn't know what he would do without her. Ben rushed to hug his daughter and kiss Annette. He looked tired. Ben was sick of one drama after another. When would it end? Or would it ever end? He helped Annette get Bethany into the car then returned to his vehicle to follow them home. Ben was so angry that he tightly clenched the steering wheel with his hands. He should call Bell and yell at her for being so stupid but it wouldn't do any good; he knew she wouldn't listen to anything he had to say.

Both Ben and Annette arrived home at the same time. They got Bethany settled in her bedroom where she fell fast asleep from the pain medication. "I can't believe it!" stated Annette, "how could a mother withhold medical attention from a child!" Annette, being a nurse knew the risks of breaking the pelvic ring. Bethany could have suffered severe damage and Bell didn't even care enough to take her to the doctor. Ben just shook his head. This bizarre behavior was something he had become accustomed to so it really didn't wasn't that shocked that Bell had not taken his daughter to the doctor.

The next day Bethany was to return home. Annette had copied the written instructions for the medical care of Bethany. She had attempted to call Bell to no avail. Bell always screened her calls and refused to answer when Annette would call. Bethany was to be taken for a follow up visit to the orthopedic physician. Annette had even listed several in the area and Bell could choose which one to call for an appointment. This didn't happen.

When Bell saw the paperwork Annette had placed in Bethany's backpack she immediately threw them in the trash. "Who does she think she is telling me what to do with my own daughter!" stated Bell. She flipped through her address book and found the number for her Chiropractor whom she called and made an appointment for Bethany. She failed to tell the office that x-rays showed a fractured pelvic ring. When she took Bethany for her appointment the child screamed in pain as the chiropractor adjusted her spine and pelvis. This continued for two more appointments when Annette and Ben found out that she had not been seen by the appropriate physician. Annette couldn't help it. She called and left Bell a scathing message for taking the girl to a chiropractor instead of an orthopedic doctor as directed. "No one could be that ignorant!" exclaimed Annette. Ben once again let Annette handle the situation because all he could think of doing is beating the hell out of Bell. He knew this would only get him locked up in jail but it gave him some comfort to think about it.

Bethany finally healed and Bell was glad. She was tired of dealing with taking her back and forth to school because she couldn't get on the bus with crutches. This meant Bell would have to get up out of bed, get dressed and drive to the school. Most days Bethany was anywhere from thirty minutes to an hour late. It was okay at first when everyone was sympathetic but the sympathy waned over time. Now the front office staff the school was making remarks to Bethany every morning that she was late. Her grades were poor too. Bethany really tried to do well in school but it was hard when she was constantly late and Bell was no help with homework at home. Bell's mental condition was getting worse so she took more pills which resulted in her sleeping most of the time. She had fallen into deep depression and didn't even bother bathing or cleaning the house. Her small dog defecated on the carpet and Bell just left it to dry before placing it in the trash. The house smelled horrible. Bethany dressed herself and ate sleeves of crackers for dinner. The girl was grateful for her weekends at her father's house; at least Annette cooked nutritious meals for her but she in turn blamed her father and Annette for her mother's condition. Ben had always made sure there was food in the refrigerator and that the house was clean. She tried to like Annette at first but she had her mother's darkness in her and all she could think about was she wanted her parents together again. She grew to despise her step mother.

Annette was finding it harder and harder to deal with Bell and her insanity. Bell was filling Bethany's head with all kinds of lies. She loved her step daughter even though the girl repeatedly told her how much she hated her and wanted her parents back together. Annette understood that all children want their parents reunited but Bethany could be extremely hateful when she was in one of her moods. She was just a child mimicking her mother so Annette couldn't blame her and believed that showing love and patience she would change her ways. Could the darkness within her mother have been inherited by the girl? At times Bethany acted very strange; talking to an imaginary friend and laughing when she saw an animal being abused on television. In fact when Annette's dog dug under the fence and escaped into the road where it was hit by a car Bethany laughed out loud at the news. Hunter was devastated and lashed out at his step sister when she laughed. No, something was just not quite right with the girl.

Chapter 13

Bell awoke with a start. Someone was knocking on her door. When she opened it she was met by a deputy who had papers in hand. "Are you Bell Cunningham?" he asked.

"Yes," replied Bell

"Then you have been served," he stated as he handed her official looking papers.

When Bell opened the envelope she found a subpoena to appear in court for a custody hearing. She couldn't believe this was happening. Ben was suing for custody of Bethany! "How dare him!" she screamed out loud. Bell was in near panic mode and didn't know what to do. She was sobbing as she called her friend from her support group and explained the situation. Her friend advised her to retain an attorney as quickly as possible. Bell had a lawyer that she had used for the divorce. She called him only to find he didn't handle custody cases but referred her to one that did. She immediately called and set up an appointment for the following day.

The next day Bell arrived at her appointment. The attorney asked several questions as he and Bell formed a plan of action. According to Bell her husband had left her penniless with a small child. Bell told the attorney that he had run away with a woman that he had been having an affair with for some time before his divorce and now the woman was trying to take her child. The attorney felt compassionate for Bell. He had heard storied like hers several times and wanted to help. He didn't know that Ben and Annette had compiled several folders of evidence that proved Bell was unfit as a mother. She had used Ben's insurance for herself and was caught but not prosecuted, had forged Ben's name for credit cards, again was caught but not prosecuted and finally did not seek medical attention when Bethany cracked her pelvis. The child had been tardy at school thirty three times in one year and Bell was currently under Department of Child and Family Services investigation for child neglect. Additionally, she had called and made false statements to the local police department accusing Ben of family violence. Luckily, he had been working at the time and had his coworkers as an alibi.

Bell felt much better after consulting an attorney. The guy seemed genuinely concerned and although he was quite pricey she felt confident that she could win the case. It would be a couple of months before she had to go to court so she decided that Bethany was not going to be allowed to visit Ben and Annette until the judge made his decision. Ben had gone too far this time and Bell was not standing for it. She never would have dreamed that Ben would try to take their daughter; this must have been Annette's idea. She had underestimated Ben's wife. She really didn't think that Annette would want to be burdened by another child so she must be doing this to impress Ben. "I hate that bitch!" thought Bell.

When Bell's attorney received that evidence from Ben's lawyer he was flabbergasted. Everything his client had told him had been a lie! She obviously was unfit! He called Bell to make her aware of the enormous amount of evidence they had against her and to suggest that she may just want to let Ben have his daughter. "You really don't want all of this aired in court," he counseled, "They will prove you're an unfit mother and it's possible you could go to jail for some of the things you've done. I would highly recommend that you just give in and let Ben have Bethany."

Bell began to cry. "I'm doing the best that I can do!" she sobbed. "What more does that woman want from me? I hate them!"

"Look Bell, this may give you a chance to straighten up and focus on yourself and get your life in order. I'm very sorry but I have to be honest with you."

"I understand," she replied, "thank you." She hung up the phone.

Bell felt like someone had just punched her in the stomach. She knew Ben would never do this to her. It was obvious to Bell that Annette made all the decisions and Ben was just going along with her. No one knew Ben better that Bell and as far as she was concerned he was still her husband and nobody could take that away. She walked into Bethany's room and again burst into tears. The little girl instantly became upset that her mother was crying. When Bell explained what Annette was doing Bethany too began to cry. "I don't want to leave you!" She wailed, "I hate Annette!" That was exactly what Bell wanted to hear. How could the court system drag a sobbing little girl away from her mother? It would be some time before their court appearance so Bell had time to work on Bethany.

Bell's anger was eating away at her like some kind of flesh eating disease. She hated Annette with a passion. She took delight in thinking of different ways she could hurt or even kill her. This woman had ruined Bell's life and she was not going to let her get away with it! Bell signed Annette up on internet dating services, entered her in any sweepstakes she could find and blasted her name all over town. She even convinced some of her friends to call Annette and tell her that Ben was cheating; anything she could do to harass her. Bell had her friends call Annette's phone and hang up several times a day until the bitch got wise and contacted the phone service. Bell was on a mission which was to make Annette's life miserable.

It was working. Annette was receiving emails from men she didn't know and when she finally figured out what was going on she had to contact the dating service to have her name removed. She received multiple phone calls a day from telemarketers from the sweepstakes that had been entered in her name. Annette was becoming very frustrated. She suspected Bell was behind it all but just couldn't prove it. When the women called to inform her that Ben was cheating she would hang up and block the caller's number so they couldn't call back. Annette even changed her phone number due to the enormous amounts of calls she would receive every day. She was sick of it! She couldn't understand how Bell had gotten away with all the illegal things she had done in the past few years.

Chapter 14

Bethany was beside herself with worry. She loved her father but she loved her mother as well. She didn't know what to believe. All she knew was now her father had another woman in his life and Bethany and her mother was left out. She really didn't hate Annette; Annette treated her well on her visits but Bell said this would not last; that Annette would change once Bethany came to live with her father. They had a beautiful home that was always clean and smelled nice. The girl had her own room and there was always plenty to eat in kitchen. She liked Hunter. It was nice to have a brother and although sometimes they fought they still had fun together. Ben told his daughter that the judge would want to speak with her. What was she supposed to say? If she said she wanted to live with her father then her mother would be upset. If she decided to stay with her mother then her dad and Annette would be upset. It was a dilemma. Bethany didn't know what to do. One thing she did know was that she was getting sick from the filthy home. The house smelled of dog feces and urine. Bethany had on more than one occasion suffered from a severe staph infection.

A few months ago Bethany had broken out in a rash all over her face. Bell had told her it was poison ivy and had smeared some medicine on the rash. Bethany went to her father's house to visit and her face became swollen and red. Her eye swelled completely closed. Annette took her to the emergency room and found that the girl had a severe case of staph infection which is highly contagious. The physician said it was the worst case he had ever seen and gave Bethany a shot along with a prescription for medication. He stated that if they had not brought the child for medical attention she could have lost sight in her eye. The infection had spread over a few hours to the rest of her body. Bethany was miserable from the itchy rash. Annette spent all weekend sanitizing her home to ensure neither Hunter of anyone else contracted the infection. Being a nurse she knew that Bell's filthy house was the probable cause for the infection. She tried not to say too much in front of Bethany but she was angry. Ben didn't seem surprised although he was concerned about his daughter.

"Annette, Bell has always had a nasty house. She used to soak clothes in the bathtub and leave them in there for weeks!" said Ben. "It was just a matter of time before someone in that house got sick. I'm surprised it hadn't happened sooner."

This just aggravated Annette. Why wasn't Ben as angry as she was? If Bell had been this bad why didn't he leave her a long time ago? She understood that he wanted to make sure his daughter was capable of taking care of herself before he left but to what extent? Bell should be in a mental institution!

Annette just couldn't believe that her step daughter lived in such conditions. It was pitiful! How could anyone stand to stay in a place like that? Annette sat Bethany down and explained in detail about the infection and how it's contracted. The poor child was finally getting some relief from the severe rash. Her eye had finally started to return to somewhat normal. Bethany begged Annette to help her. She loved her mother but she didn't want to suffer like this again. Unfortunately, Annette had to return the girl home but promised that it wouldn't be for long. The court date was just a few weeks away and Annette was hopeful that she and Ben would get custody of Bethany.

The day finally came. Court was to begin at nine o'clock sharp. Ben and Annette were the first to show up. They sat in the back of courtroom and waited. Bell and a group of women from her "support group" entered the courtroom just a few minutes before nine. Bell was crying while her friends were hovering around her comforting her. They put on quite a show . . . Bell would sob for a while then close her eyes as if praying. Before the judge entered the room both lawyers motioned for their clients to follow them to the conference room. Bell's attorney stated that Bell would give up custody without a fight. She didn't want to appear before the judge. "I bet she doesn't," Annette thought sarcastically. Bell didn't say a word and without looking at anyone left the room in tears. Bethany would be delivered to Ben and Annette's house before five o'clock by one of Bell's friends. Ben was given full custody of his daughter. The couple rejoiced at the news. When they left the courthouse they saw Bell parked at the end of the entrance. She held her hand out the window and held up her middle finger in anger. Bell had lost custody of her only child and was out to seek revenge.

Bell returned home exhausted with rage. They had taken her baby girl from her. Additionally, she wouldn't be receiving the twelve hundred dollars a month in child support. She needed that money! She didn't even want to see Bethany so she called her friend and asked if she would just go ahead and take her to Ben's house. She wasn't going to send anything with the girl anyhow. They could buy her clothes and shoes and toys. Everything of Bethany's was staying right here at her home. She had bought the stuff and was keeping it! Annette and Ben made good money so they could buy her things since they think that can care for the child better than her own mother. What could Bell tell her friends? That she was unfit as a mother? No, she would have to come up with something else . . . maybe that she had become too sick to care for a child . . . yes that was it. Bell would stay in hiding for a few days until someone called to check. She could then tell them how sick she was and that she had sent Bethany to live with her father until she got well.

Bethany arrived at Annette and Ben's as planned. Annette had spent days painting and fixing up the room so Bethany would feel as comfortable as possible. She knew that little girl was going to miss her mother but this was the best place for her. A child could not continue to live in filth with some crazy woman even if it was her mother. Bethany was surprised that her room looked so good and gave Annette a big hug. "Thank you, Annette," she stated. She had games, stuffed animals, and even a television in her room that overlooked the swimming pool. Bethany had never had anything like this before. She slept in this same room when she visited but didn't think of it as her own. Now, this room was hers. It was clean with freshly laundered sheets on the bed. No more cockroaches crawling on her at night like at her mother's house. No more getting herself up in the mornings and being late for school. Maybe this wasn't going to be bad at all in fact; maybe this was going to be great. Although she would miss her mother desperately she could visit every other weekend.

Annette was glad Bethany liked her room. She knew they all had a long way to go before the girl would settle in but Annette was sure that day would come. What Annette didn't realize that things would become much worse before it got better? She had to register Bethany in the new school which meant she had to withdraw her from her old one. When Annette arrived to remove the girl the staff at the front desk was quite surprised that Ben had actually won custody. Annette was completing the necessary paperwork when she read that Bethany was enrolled as a special needs child. The papers showed that the girl was dyslexic, had ADD, and suffered from delayed mental development yet there were no corresponding paperwork from the pediatrician. This was the first time she had heard anything about Bethany's problems so she searched for the physician's statements and found none. When Annette asked the school counselor about it she told her that the girl's mother had insisted that Bethany had been diagnosed by her pediatrician but never received official paperwork. She said Bell was supposed to have the documents sent from the pediatrician's office but she guessed no one ever followed up. Annette knew that this was against state regulations and couldn't comprehend that they would take Bell's word for anything as crazy as she was and actually placed Bethany in the special education class. On the other hand, what kind of mother would make up stuff like this about their only child? Had everyone gone mad? Why did they believe that insane bitch? Annette was angry when she finally left the school. At least Bethany was out of special education and would be enrolled in a decent school and regular classes and she would arrive at school on time.

Chapter 15

Bell decided to visit Bethany at school for lunch. When she arrived and saw her daughter she began to sob causing a huge scene. Bethany was embarrassed as Bell continued to wail yelling at the girl, "Why did you leave me? What have I done to deserve this? How could you hurt your own mother? You have betrayed me, Bethany!"

Bethany dropped her head. She wished she could just crawl in a hole. Her mother was out of control. Bell had somewhat composed herself as she reached into her purse for a tissue. To Bethany's horror a cockroach crawled out of her mother's purse and onto the cafeteria table. Bethany's friends squealed in fright and ran away from the table leaving their lunch. A teacher came over to see what was going on. Bell lied and said the cockroach crawled up the table from the floor. Bethany's friend promptly told her she was lying and moved to a different table. Bethany was devastated. She asked her mother to leave. Bell started crying again and told her daughter how hateful and disrespectful she was being. The teacher escorted them both to the front office to get them out of the situation. Bell left the building crying and Bethany had to sit in the office until she calmed down. She was ashamed to face her friends after her mother's fiasco.

When Bethany got home she told Annette and Ben what had happened. Ben wrote a letter to the school asking that Bell not be allowed to have lunch with Bethany again. Bethany was so upset she didn't want to return to school. Her friends had made all manner of fun of her and her mother. It was hard enough for the girl attending a new school and trying to make new friends. Now Bell had made things worse for her. What was she thinking?

Bell was livid the next time she came to school to have lunch with her daughter. The receptionist told her that Bethany's father had requested that she not be allowed at the school. "How dare him!" she screamed at the lady. "He can't do this!" She immediately called her attorney who in turn verified that Ben was within his legal rights. Bell couldn't believe it! She couldn't even go see her own daughter at school. "This had to be Annette's doing!" she thought. "Ben would never do anything like this to me."

She returned home in a fury. She would get Annette if it was the last thing she did! What could she do to make that woman pay? Bell heard a knock at the front door. "What now?" she thought. When she opened the door she was served with a subpoena for child support. She was floored. What the hell? Her ex-husband was suing her for child support! Ben had told her she didn't have to ever pay child support; she could get her best friend to lie and say she had heard him say it! Again, this had to be Annette. What more did this bitch want from her? She took her husband and her only child and now she wants money too! "We'll see about that!" she thought. "I'll blow that bitch's head off before I pay a dime of child support!"

Bell had postponed the child support hearing for as long as she could. The day finally came and Bell got up on the stand and lied through her teeth. She sobbed as she told the judge how broke she was and how she was disabled and couldn't work. She told the court she volunteered at the local nursing home. Annette had already given the case worker Bell's work phone number along with the name of her supervisor. The case worker called and verified that Bell did indeed work there for payment although she only worked nine hours per week. When the judge found out that Bell had lied he immediately ruled in favor of Ben. Bell would have to pay the minimum amount for child support. Bell told the court that she couldn't afford the amount. The judge angrily told her to get a job as he quickly got up and headed to his chamber. Bell just sat in disbelief as everyone cleared the courtroom. Theirs was the last case to be heard so she sat all alone for quite some time before she was asked to leave by the bailiff. She couldn't even speak she was so flabbergasted by the judge's ruling. She hadn't even had a chance to tell him that Ben had promised never to make her pay.

Now she had to pay Ben? This was unreal! Annette and Ben sure had a lot of nerve!

Ben and Annette were pleased. Bell didn't have to pay a lot of money for child support but at least she was made to do something. She had refused to buy anything for Bethany since she had moved in with Ben, not even a pencil for school. When Bethany needed something Bell told her to ask Annette. Annette didn't mind spending money on Bethany but she did want Bell to act like a parent and help in some small way; any way for that matter. Bell wouldn't even buy the child ice cream when she came to visit. She told her daughter that she couldn't afford it now that Annette had made Ben sue her for child support. It was always Annette's fault in Bell's eyes. Ben would never treat the mother of his child like this if it weren't for Annette. She obviously had some kind of hold on him. One way or the other Bell was determined to break that hold. She vowed to get her husband and child back.

Ben was tired of dealing with his ex-wife. He hated her so much that he refused to even speak to her. Every time they had a conversation Bell would try to file a complaint with the local police department claiming he threatened her so he no longer took her calls. Annette, on the other hand, handled any and all conversations with Bell. Most of the time the conversations would end in a shouting match with Annette hanging up on her. Bell would insist on speaking with Ben and Annette would explain over and over why that wouldn't happen. Bell just didn't get it so she tried to send notes to Ben via Bethany. Annette would intercept them at Ben's request. Finally Ben ordered Bethany to stop carrying notes from her mother. She complied even at the protest of her mother.

Bethany was torn between her mother and father. She loved them both. Maybe it really was Annette's fault that her parents broke up; at least that's what her mother constantly tells her. Was it true that her she and her parents would still be one big happy family if Annette hadn't interfered? Was her father really mesmerized by this woman? Bethany was so confused she didn't know what to believe. What she did know was that she wanted her parents back together again and she wanted Annette to go away. She wished Annette no harm; she just wanted her to leave.

None of Bell's plans had worked. Annette was still with her husband and Bell couldn't stand it. She never would have dreamed that Ben would remarry and move on with his life. Ben and Annette had built a very large home with an in ground swimming pool, new cars and from what Bethany had told her they were both making a good paycheck from their jobs. Bell had been left with a run down, small two bedroom house from when she and Ben were married. It had no central heating or air conditioning; just space heaters and window units. The porch was falling apart and Ben wouldn't come by to repair it. Bell's old car wasn't running well and again, Ben was no help. It seemed to her that Ben had abandoned her and didn't care what happened. This part was true . . . Ben didn't care what happened to his ex-wife. He would be happy if she fell off the face of the earth. Bell refused to work more than nine or ten hours a week and had been living off of the money she had scammed and stored in safe deposit boxes while living like a homeless person. She never bought groceries although she ate well at the soup kitchens and church gatherings. She hadn't purchased new clothes in years; all of her clothes came from the thrift store. Bell's appearance had declined even more. She looked twenty years older that she actually was, only bathed weekly, and wore several layers of clothing with holes in various places. She didn't own any shoes other than flip flops that showed untrimmed toenails and calloused feet. She was grossly obese and in poor health both physically and mentally.

Chapter 16

Annette had worked all night and arrived home exhausted. Ben had left early to drop off Hunter and Bethany at school on his way to work. She had the house all to herself. She popped a bagel in the toaster and poured a glass of orange juice and picked up the stack of mail from the day before. She saw an envelope from a mortgage company addressed to Ben and Bell. The letter stated that Bell's mortgage was in Ben's name and was sixty days in arrears. The statement showed that Ben was being charged over fourteen hundred dollars for Bell's house payment and responsible for the full one hundred thousand dollars. Annette was furious. When Ben came home from work Annette was unable to control her anger. "Why is your name still on Bell's mortgage?" she demanded. Ben had just walked in the door and was bewildered. "What are you talking about?" he asked. Annette showed him the letter from the mortgage company. By this time she had calmed somewhat but now Ben was angry. He would call their attorney first thing in the morning and get this straightened out.

Their attorney requested the paperwork on Bell's home. She had apparently forged his name to the documents years ago without Ben's knowledge. A letter was sent to her by the attorney that threatened a lawsuit if she didn't have Ben's name removed from her mortgage. Ben also filed a report with the local police who once again did absolutely nothing. They stated that it was a civil matter and Ben needed to contact an attorney. Bell finally called Annette a few weeks later and told her that she had paid off the house and Ben's name had been removed. Ben received a call from

Bell's attorney who had him come to his office to sign the appropriate papers to ensure that only Bell's name was on the paperwork. Annette and Ben were relieved but still couldn't believe that Bell had gotten by with criminal activity again. This woman could actually murder someone and get by with it claiming she was insane! The couple didn't realize just how true this was.

Bethany was getting used to living with her dad and Annette. She missed her mother still but life was easier in her new home. She really wished that Annette would leave so she and her father could live alone. He would let her do anything she wanted if it weren't for Annette and Bethany would get all the attention. The girl was like her mother in that she wanted all the attention all of the time. As it was now Annette was getting most of the attention and then there's Hunter poking his nose in Bethany's business all the time. How could Bethany get the attention she deserved with these two people taking up most of Ben's time? Ben was her father not Hunter's but yet Ben seemed to be interested in doing "guy" things with his step son. Bethany didn't know that Ben had adopted Hunter. She realized it when Hunter began using Ben's last name on his school work. Bethany was livid! Her mother had told her that Ben had always wanted a little boy and now he had one. Oh how they would pay for this! She was supposed to be her daddy's only child!

When Bell picked up Bethany for her visit the girl told her mother all about the adoption. "See! I told you so!" stated Bell, "Your father now has the son he always wanted. Pretty soon he will forget all about you" Bethany had a look of horror on her face. How could her father do this to her? Bell wouldn't give it a rest. She went on and on about how Ben was slowly replacing Bell and Bethany with Hunter and Annette. "Just wait," Bell said hatefully, "Annette will change and become the wicked step mother. You'll wish you was living back home with me!" Bethany started to cry as Bell smiled. This is just want Bell wanted. Now maybe Bethany will go along with the plan to break Annette and Ben apart. When they arrived at Bell's house the girl had to hold her nose until she got used to the stench. The house was in disarray and cockroaches scattered when they turned on the lights. Spoiled food was left in the refrigerator along with trash piled several bags high in the corner of the kitchen. Bethany sighed as she started to clean. She couldn't stay in this messy place all weekend. Bell headed straight for the bedroom to take a nap. At least Bethany cleaned when she came to visit. Maybe she would take her somewhere fun tomorrow . . . Bethany dragged the trash to the curb and vomited when she saw maggots crawling out of one of the trash bags. How could her mother stand to live here? Was she so depressed that she didn't even clean a little? This was Annette and her father's fault. They had caused her mother to become so depressed that she didn't even take care of herself! Bethany hated them both. She cleaned until the wee hours of the morning when she finally decided to sleep on the couch. She left the light on because she was afraid of the cockroaches but was so exhausted that she fell asleep within minutes. She awoke and felt like her head was on fire she was itching so badly. Her mother looked at her scalp and said that she had a very bad case of dandruff. She gave Bethany some medicated shampoo and told her to wash her hair.

Bethany was still scratching her head when she arrived home at Ben and Annette's. She ran upstairs after saying hello and stayed in her room. By now her scalp was bleeding from scratching her head all weekend. Annette came into her room to make sure the girl was alright. When she inspected Bethany's hair and scalp she called Ben upstairs to see. Bethany had an extremely bad case of head lice. Ben ran to the store for medicine but it didn't give the child any relief. Annette took Bethany to the doctor the next morning and got some prescription medication to kill the bugs. Bethany continued to get head lice every time she visited her mother for the next eight months. Annette was at her wits end. She was constantly decontaminating the house only for Bethany to bring bugs home again. It was not the child's fault; it was Bell's nasty house. Annette called Bell to reason with her but the conversation just ended in an argument. Ben and Annette called the Department of Family and Children's Services and refused to allow Bethany to visit her mother until she cleaned her house. Bell complied only after Department of Family and Children's Services became involved. They required Bell to show proof of pest extermination and made several visits to her home before they allowed Bethany to return. Bell was embarrassed and angry. Did Ben and Annette think they could run her life? They couldn't tell her what she could and couldn't do in her own home! She went along with them this time but never again! She didn't care if they let Bethany visit or not!

Chapter 17

It was a beautiful warm spring day when Bethany and Hunter decided to take a walk in the woods. Both children had been getting along quite well lately so they thought a picnic would be ideal. Bethany packed sandwiches while Hunter gathered a couple cans of drinks. They placed the food in their backpacks and headed down the trail. They had several acres that surrounded their home so Ben had cut trails throughout the woods. After a few minutes of walking they came upon a small turtle beside a stream. Bethany promptly flipped the turtle on its back and placed a heavy rock on the turtle's belly. Bethany laughed as its little legs struggled to get free. Hunter was horrified. "What are you doing?" he said loudly, "The turtle will die!"

"I know," Bethany quietly replied, "Let's watch it!" Bethany felt the darkness well up inside her and it felt great. She welcomed the warm tingling feeling and wanted more.

Hunter was instantly mad as he shoved the girl away and freed the poor creature. Little did the boy know that this was history repeating itself? Bethany's mother had done this same exact thing when she was a child. Hunter made sure the little turtle was far away from Bethany before he returned home. The picnic was off. He was sick to his stomach from his sister's behavior. How could anyone be this cruel? That poor turtle wasn't hurting anyone and what kind of miserable death would it have suffered at the hands of his sister? He would never return to the woods with her again. Bethany smiled to herself. She loved to shock people especially

Hunter. She gained attention from doing shocking or stupid things since other children were so gullible. She once held a kitten under water until it stopped breathing at her mom's house in order to get even with the neighbor girl who had called her ugly. She had told the girl that she would do the same to her if she told anyone. As far as Bethany knew the girl never told on her.

Bell would awake every day seething with anger which lasted all day. She hated Ben but she hated Annette even more. She had to find a way to get even with them. She wished she could torture them until they died! Her life was ruined and it was their fault! Bell had always been overweight but she was grossly obese and feeling very sorry for herself. Her friends begged her to lose weight and join a gym. They insisted she would feel better about herself if she just tried a little. Bell wanted no part of it. She loved wallowing in self pity and actually enjoyed the anger deep inside her. She would spend days contemplating on what she could do to make Ben and Annette's life hell. She had to be careful though, they were pretty quick to pick up on her scams and lies. Bell had bad mouthed the couple all over town but people were wise to Bell's craziness and didn't pay her too much attention. The few people that would listen were very sympathetic to Bell's plight and she enjoyed spinning her tale of woe. Bell would fall asleep every night thinking of ways to get even with Ben and Annette.

She came up with a plan. She would get one of her closest friends to call Annette and claim to be Ben's girlfriend. She had only one friend that she could trust enough for a job like this . . . Donna Evans. Donna was just as screwed up as Bell so they got along just fine. She called and explained what she wanted done and Donna was more than happy to do it. She would write down everything so as not to forget the important things.

Annette's phone rang just as she was leaving work the next morning. "Hello, Is this Annette?" a woman's voice asked.

"Yes, who's this?" Annette replied

"I'm a friend of your husband and I can't stand the guilt anymore. I wanted to let you know that we've been having an affair for several months and we love each other very much. I'm sorry you had to find out this way but I think you should know." The caller stated.

Annette didn't hesitate in her reply, "Go to hell! I don't believe it you stupid bitch and don't call me again!" Annette slammed the phone shut. "I know Bell was behind this!" she thought. "And I've had enough!" Annette immediately called Ben. She wasn't mad at her husband, she trusted him completely. She was extremely angry at Bell. The caller didn't realize that Annette had heard her voice before when she was picking up Bethany. Donna had called Annette on Bell's behalf to let her know that Bethany was going to be late returning home from a visit with her mother. Ben was furious. This had gone too far. Bell was never going to leave them alone and he didn't know how to stop her. She was making their life miserable and that's exactly what she wanted to do. Why wouldn't his ex-wife realize that he was never coming back to her and move on with her life? He just didn't understand why she was determined to cause problems. Thank God Annette didn't believe this caller! He loved his wife dearly and would never do anything to hurt her.

When Donnas' phone went dead after her conversation with Annette she promptly called Bell. "I don't think she believed me, Bell." She said. Donna gave her the replay of the conversation. Bell was furious. "You should have been more convincing!" she yelled. "You screwed it up!" Donna was shocked. She was trying to help her friend get her husband back and this is the thanks she gets? "I'm sorry Bell but you know I was lying and it's hard for me to be convincing. Next time don't ask me for any favors!" Donna slammed the phone onto its receiver.

What kind of hold did Annette have over Ben? This was the perfect plan until Donna messed it up! Bell had dreamed of the day when Ben would come home with his little girl and beg Bell to forgive him. She would agree and they would live happily ever after. Maybe even have another child! Bell smiled at the thought of living with Ben again. He had taken care of her before so he had to have loved her at one time. He could find that love again if she could just get Annette out of the picture.

Chapter 18

B ell received word that one of her cousins had committed suicide. She hadn't seen the man since they were children but this would be the perfect opportunity to receive some sympathy. She called her support group and got the ball rolling. She managed to muster up some tears and when the first person arrived at her door to bring food she began her drama. She sobbed and cried pretending to be terrible hurt by the death. Her neighbors brought food and even offered to stay with her throughout the night. She acted so devastated that they considered contacting Bell's physician for something to help her rest. This act lasted for three full days until the funeral. Bell really put on a show then. She actually pretended to faint during the ceremony. They called an ambulance to take her to the hospital . . . where Annette had picked up a day shift.

This had certainly not been in Bell's plan. When the ambulance crew brought Bell in to the emergency room they placed her on a stretcher in the hall. Annette walked up and couldn't believe her eyes. There lay Bell pretending to go in and out of consciousness. Annette realized this was not a good situation to be in since both women hated each other so much. She called one of the other nurses over to take care of Bell. When Bell realized that the emergency room staff was not in a big hurry to rush to her side she began to yell obscenities. The staff tried to calm her down but to no avail. She demanded to see the physician who was with a critical patient. Annette walked over to Bell and took control of the situation. "Look Bell, these people are trying to help you but you have to calm down." Annette said calmly. Bell had lost all control and reached into her purse and pulled out a knife. "I'll cut your ass, bitch!" she screamed. Security had arrived in time to witness the pending attack. They immediately restrained Bell and removed the knife from her hand. The police were called. As soon as Bell was cleared from the hospital she was taken to jail for aggravated assault. She made bond a couple of days later and was released until her court date. Bell had to find a good attorney. She didn't intend for things to get so out of hand but it really did feel good to see the look on Annette's face when she thought she was going to be stabbed. Bell smiled. She would have loved to stick that knife deep in Annette's chest and watch her bleed to death. She imagined the bloody, frothy sputum gurgling from Annette's lungs just before she suffocated from her own blood and died.

Bell finally found an attorney to represent her. Their defense would be extreme stress and temporary insanity. Given Bell's mental background, attending her cousin's funeral as well as the torment of seeing her husband's concubine in the emergency room should prove their insanity plea and result in probation. The attorney told Bell he didn't believe she would do any time in prison. He was correct. The district attorney's office allowed Bell to plea to a reduced charge in return for five years probation since she was a first time offender.

Annette and Ben were shocked! Bell had pulled a knife, threatened Annette and had gotten by with it! What kind of justice system did they have? Was the entire world going crazy? They were sure the case would go to court and Bell would have to spend at least some time in jail. They could hire an attorney but that would cost thousands of dollars. Unbelievable! What would Bell do next? Her mental stability was obviously growing worse.

Bell awoke the day after court in a very good mood. She had beaten the system. Being insane wasn't so bad after all. She could pretty much do as she wished and get by with it. She decided to focus more on the aging elderly couple she had been taking care of. She got dressed and drove down the street for a visit. They were excited to see Bell. They rarely had company so this was a treat. She visited for several hours before she brought up the subject of finances. She had been paying their bills and managing their finances. She told them it would be much easier for her if they just gave her power of attorney. After careful consideration they agreed. Bell would have her attorney draw up the papers and she would pick them up in a couple of days to drive them to the attorney's office. She would have full control of the couple's money. She would next have their deed to their home transferred to her name. "This is so easy!" she thought. She will soon have three homes in addition to more money. What a day!

A few days later Bell picked up the elderly couple and drove them to her attorney's office. They readily signed away all their rights to Bell. They trusted her completely. She had been nothing but nice and helpful to them since they became sick with terminal diseases. To them Bell was a Godsend. The couple had children but they lived far away and were busy all the time. Their kids didn't even know that they had been sick so they had no idea that their parents were being scammed by Bell. Now all Bell had to do is sit back and wait.

Chapter 19

Bell was lonely. She decided it was time to find a man so she signed up for an online dating service. It worked pretty well. She was asked out on lots of dates; however, she was never called back by any of the men for a second date. She had been seeing this man from the local grocery store. Although they had only met for lunch a few times maybe they could take their friendship to a new level. She called her friend and he agreed to meet her for dinner.

Tim was a nice enough guy who worked at the local grocery store stocking products. Although he didn't find Bell attractive she was fun to hang out with. Tim was not a handsome man and had a very limited education. He was several years older than Bell and lived alone with his cat in a small apartment close to the nursing home where she worked. He and Bell made the perfect couple because he was not intelligent enough to see through her little schemes and lies and although Bell made it through high school she was not very bright so the two of them got along well.

Bell and Tim dated frequently. She like the fact that he believed everything she told him and was very sympathetic regarding her plight. Tim would do anything Bell asked him no matter what is was and would follow Bell around like a little puppy. Tim took on a second job because Bell complained that she didn't have enough money. He would hand her his signed paycheck to spend as she pleased. All Bell had to do is sleep with him about once a month and the old man was happy. He didn't even mind her nastiness. Tim wasn't used to being around women so he was ecstatic that Bell gave him any attention at all.

Bethany finally came back to visit her mother. Bell had to clean the house before her daughter arrived thanks to Annette. She had planned to take Bethany to the airport with her today. Tim was flying to Florida to visit his family so Bell planned to drive him to the airport. They were a couple of hours early so they decided to ride the airport train for awhile. Bell and Tim were cozy holding hands and laughing while not paying attention to Bethany. They jumped on the train and as the doors closed they didn't see the girl with them. She was looking at the artwork on the walls and didn't see her mother and Tim get on the train. The train took off leaving Bethany standing in the breezeway alone. When she realized what had happened she began to panic and cry. She found a lady in uniform and told her that she was lost. Meanwhile, Bell didn't seem concerned. "We'll just ride the train around the airport and pick her up where we left her." Bell stated. Tim seemed okay with her logic and wasn't worried about a little girl alone in the largest airport in the nation. The lady in the uniform actually worked for the airlines and took Bethany to the security desk. "No one has reported missing a child." The officer said. "Stay here with me until we find your parents." When Bell and Tim finally reached the area where they had left Bethany she wasn't there. Bell still didn't seem concerned as they continued to search for her. During this time Bethany called Ben who spoke with the security officer. "Sir, your daughter has been at my station for the last forty five minutes and no one has reported her missing." The officer stated. "I'll be there in thirty minutes!" Ben replied as he rushed to his care to go get his daughter.

When Ben arrived at the airport he was frantic. How had Bethany gotten lost at the airport? Where was Bell? He met the officer at the security desk where he found Bethany eating a candy bar and sipping a drink. She was happy to see her father. The officer explained to Ben what had happened and said he could take his daughter home. During their conversation Bell and Tim came to the desk to report Bethany missing. By this time more than an hour had passed without notification the Bell had lost her daughter.

"I'm taking Bethany home!" Ben declared.

Bell started to say something but both Ben and the security guard gave her a look that hushed her completely. Maybe she should just wait until later to explain to Ben what had happened. He looked pretty mad at this point. Bethany quickly waved to her mother and left with Ben. How stupid could a person be? This girl could have been raped and assaulted in a huge airport like this.

When Annette heard the news she just couldn't grasp what had happened. She knew Bell was crazy but why didn't she immediately report Bethany missing? Didn't she care what could happen to her own daughter? How could Ben have ever been married to someone like this? It was just too much for Annette to comprehend.

Bethany was exhausted and went to bed early after her big day at the airport. She was grateful that her father came to pick her up. She didn't understand why she couldn't continue her visit with her mother but she guessed it really didn't matter. Her father had been so angry he didn't have much to say on the way home so she didn't even bother to ask. She hadn't even spoken to Annette which was not unusual since she really didn't like her step mother. She only spoke when she needed something or if Annette were to ask her a question. She could talk to her father for hours; in fact if Annette wasn't taking up all of his time Bethany could enjoy doing things with her dad; but Annette was always there with him along with Hunter.

Hunter pretty much stayed to himself. He played video games and drew pictures since he was quite the artist. He spent hours in his room drawing and painting. Sometimes Bethany would come to watch. He really didn't mind unless she was in one of her moods then he would demand she leave. He really cared for his step sister but he didn't understand her. She was always doing weird and mean things; just like the incident with the turtle. Sometimes he would hear her talking to herself. When asked she would deny it. Hunter had noticed that Bethany would destroy things on purpose and claim it was an accident or blame him. On one particular occasion she carved her name into Annette's car but became very defensive when asked about the damage. She claimed Hunter did it to get her into trouble so both children were punished.

Bell decided to get Bethany a dog. She searched the paper for free puppies and found a little terrier that was begin given away to a good home. She called the owners and arranged to pick up the animal. When she got the puppy home she began having some of her old feelings return. She was sitting on her bed sewing a hole in her blouse. She looked at her needle and then at the puppy. She became overwhelmed as she called the small dog to her. As she held its collar firmly she shoved the needled deep into its fur until she penetrated the skin. The puppy yelped in pain as it struggled to get away. Bell felt powerful as she stuck the needle in again. This time the shrill yelp of the puppy was so loud that she let go of its collar. Bell felt alive! She knew the penalty for animal cruelty was great so she had to be careful but this was more fun than torturing baby birds or turtles. The puppy cowered in the corner as Bell walked over to comfort the animal. The bleeding was minimal but it wasn't blood that thrilled Bell; it was the ability to cause extreme pain in a helpless creature. Even her own sister didn't squeal this loud when she died. Bell gave the dog a treat as she put it in the kennel for the night. Oh what fun she was going to have with this dog!

The next month or so the animal was tortured almost daily. Bell reveled in the power she felt every time it yelped in pain. You couldn't tell by looking at the dog that it had suffered multiple penetrating holes in its skin because of it's long thick fur. The puppy hid under the sofa most of the day trying to avoid Bell and her evil ways. She would eventually find it and punish the dog for not coming directly to her when she called. The poor animal didn't understand; all it knew was that life was a living hell. Bell kept the dog for a few months and soon grew tired of the animal's constant whimpering so she opened the door and allowed it to run away. She kicked it hard as it passed through the doorway. The frightened little puppy saw the opportunity to get away and didn't stop running until it was near exhaustion. A passerby saw the small dog and picked it up thinking it was a stray.

Tim was working so much now that Bell didn't get to see much of him. At least he would come by Friday evenings long enough to drop off his paycheck then head to his second job. This had become the routine for the past several months. Tim didn't seem to mind working but he wanted to spend more time with Bell. She loved it! Here was a man working for her like a slave and she didn't have to do much in return and he was very rarely around to bother her. Bethany only came to visit about once a month so Bell had plenty of time to do as she pleased. She would get up on Saturday mornings and drive around the high end neighborhoods to rummage in their trash. She found all kinds of useful items that she took home. She kept some of the items while others she sold at yard sales.

Chapter 20

Annette suffered from severe asthma. She hadn't had an episode for a couple of years but this year seemed to make up for it. She suffered from two attacks in the last couple of months. Fortunately, she was able to use her inhaler and get relief. She didn't feel well today and called in sick from work. She thought maybe she was coming down with something but wasn't sure. She was achy and feverish. Bethany had sprayed an extreme amount of perfume in her room before she left for school and Annette started to have difficulty in breathing so she searched for her many inhalers placed in various areas of the house. She pulled an aerosol inhaler from the kitchen drawer and attempted to use it. It was empty. She went into the living room and found another one but it too was empty. Annette felt an onset of panic since she knew all her strategically placed medicines should have been full. If she didn't find an inhaler with medicine she would soon die. Annette was struggling to breathe as she became pale and then blue around her lips. She stumbled to her bedroom and found yet another inhaler in her bedside table . . . it too was empty. The room started to spin as she gasped take a breath. Annette reached for the phone and dialed 911 just before she passed out. When she finally regained consciousness she was in the emergency room and felt like hell. Ben had been called and was feverishly pacing outside her door. The nurse in the room let out a sigh of relief she Annette opened her eyes. "We thought we had lost you," she stated. "You weren't breathing when the ambulance brought you in here." Annette tried to speak but the nurse hushed her, "Don't try to talk right now, Annette," she said. "Save your energy." When Ben saw that his wife was awake he burst into the room and rushed to Annette's side. "Thank God!" he exclaimed. "I've been so worried. If anything ever happened to you I don't think could survive." Annette smiled at him as she drifted off to sleep again.

When the doctor came in the room he asked Ben to step into the conference area with him so they could talk. Ben followed and listened intently as the doctor proceeded to speak. "The paramedics told me that they found several inhalers about the house and all of them were empty. I know Annette well enough to know she would never have allowed this to happen. Ben, something's going on and although it's none of my business I feel you need to know." "Thanks," replied Ben who appeared to be in the state of shock. "I'll find out what's happened."

Ben returned to Annette's room and found her awake and sitting up on the stretcher. Her color had returned to normal and she was breathing much better. She would get to go home shortly. Annette was happy to see Ben. She didn't remember passing out but she remembered trying to find her medication. "Ben," she said, "I don't know what happened! I am positive that every one of those inhalers was full and when I tried them they were all empty. Someone did this on purpose!"

"Annette, we will figure it out but not right now. What's important is for you to get well," said Ben.

"I've never been so frightened in my life," she replied softly.

The nurse came into the room to release Annette from the hospital. "The doctor has ordered you to take a few days off and get your strength back. We'll see you next week at work."

"Thank you," replied Annette.

Ben drove his wife home as he vowed to get to the bottom of this. Someone had sabotaged his wife and he was determined to find the culprit. When the couple arrived home they checked ever inhaler in the house. Every single one had been emptied. No one else had been in their home with the exception of Bethany and Hunter. It was possible that one of the children was playing with an inhaler and sprayed the medication out but not ALL of the inhalers. This was done purposely. Ben was angry and hurt that anyone would want his wife to die. He knew Bethany didn't like Annette at times but it was hard for him to believe that his little girl could be so evil. Surely she wasn't capable of trying to kill someone; she was just a child. Ben couldn't even comprehend that his own daughter could be responsible for trying to kill his wife.

Annette, on the other hand, was sure. Hunter knew that importance of her medicine and would never touch it. Bethany knew the importance as well. Both children had been told what could happen if Annette didn't have access to her asthma medication. She had been very clear when she talked to the children about it. Someone had deliberately emptied her inhalers and she was sure that person was Bethany. How could she discuss this with Ben? This was his only daughter whom he loved dearly.

When Hunter and Bethany returned home from school Ben and Annette sat both children down to discuss the day's happenings. Both children firmly denied touching the medication. Bethany appeared hurt by the insinuation and blamed the pest control man who happened to be in the house a few days prior. Ben hadn't thought of that but Annette was convinced it was still Bethany. "I love you, Annette," stated Bethany, "I would never do anything to harm you." Annette could tell that Ben really wanted to believe his daughter and now this revelation had placed doubt in his mind that Bethany was indeed responsible.

"Just forget it!" Annette stated and abruptly left the room. She knew the girl was responsible and it infuriated her that Bethany acted so innocent and concerned. The only thing the child was concerned about was her own self.

"Wait!" Ben exclaimed as he followed his wife to the bedroom. "Annette, you can't really think that our own child had something to do with this! I know Bethany has a lot of issues but I don't believe she would actually try to hurt you."

"Ben," Annette said calmly, "I don't want to hurt your feelings so the best thing we can do is to get past today and move forward. I have my own opinion and you have yours so let's just leave it at that."

Ben dropped his head not knowing what to say. He loved his wife but he loved his daughter as well. He was torn between believing his daughter and believing his wife. He didn't know what to think. This was a nightmare.

Ben later found his daughter in her room crying. "Daddy, you know I would just die before I did anything to hurt Annette. Why doesn't she believe me?"

"Annette has just had a horrible day, sweetie." He replied. "Give her some time and everything will be okay." He gently kissed his daughter on the cheek. "Now get some sleep."

Bethany nodded her head and wiped the tears from her eyes. As soon as Ben closed her door she began to smile. "He's so easy to fool," she thought. "If those stupid paramedics hadn't come so quickly I would have my daddy all to myself." Bethany snuggled under the covers and closed her eyes. She softly giggled at the surprised look on Annette's face when she told her she loved her. Her mother would be so proud!

The next morning Annette set off to the hardware store. She bought several metal boxes with locks, placed her inhalers inside, and placed them all over the house. She slid the key to the locks on a chain to wear around her neck. She would never go through the horror again, she vowed. She also put some of the medication in secret hiding places just in case. Annette worried what her step daughter would do next along with the safety of Hunter. She could never tell Ben her feelings. Bethany acted so sweet and polite in front of her father but appeared to be a totally different child when he wasn't around.

Bethany went to visit Bell and told her how she had been accused of taking Annette's medication. Bell was furious. "I told you she wasn't the person you thought she was going to be," said Bell. "That woman is evil! Stay away from her as much as you can." Bell thought it was a shame that help arrived to Annette so quickly. She didn't care if Bethany had been responsible or not; she would have done the same thing if she could. Bell hated Annette. She wished the woman would have died.

Bell and her daughter had a wonderful weekend. They went to the zoo and finished the day at the park. Bell never really liked the park but she found she could meet lonely elderly people there and befriend them. She had pretty much financially depleted the old couple down the street so she was on the lookout for another victim. She had been talking to a very sweet elderly woman, Ms. Beasley, who didn't have any children or family. The old lady was lonely and welcomed chatting with Bell at the park. Ms. Beasley was a retired nurse who had squirreled away thousands of dollars over her lifetime. She lived alone and had already divulged her entire life history to Bell. This was Bell's lucky day! Ms. Beasley was at the park in hopes of seeing Bell. The two women talked and the old woman invited Bell to her home. This was the beginning of a new relationship.

Bell began visiting the woman about every other day. She went shopping for her, cooked her meals, and did household chores. The old woman was very grateful and told Bell that she thought of her as if she were her own daughter. This is what Bell was hoping for . . . another sucker. As the months passed Bell finally convinced Ms. Beasley to let her handle all of the old woman's affairs. Legal papers were signed and Bell had another income . . . scamming cash from the woman's accounts.

Bell began thinking about what Bethany had told her. If only Annette hadn't been able to call 911. Bell enjoyed the mental picture of Annette gasping for air as she turned blue then becoming unresponsive. "I just wish I had been a fly on the wall to see it!" she thought. It would have only been better if Bell's hands were around Annette's neck! Just the thought of Annette struggling for air was enough to make Bell smile. She really hated that woman and would do anything in her power to hurt her. She had to think of something she could do to get even with Annette taking her husband and child away from her. It was just a matter of time before she would come up with something . . . then it hit her like a brick. What better way to get to Annette than through her precious little boy, Hunter. Bell would have to figure out the details but at least it was a sure fire plan.

Chapter 21

Annette hadn't been feeling well. She had changed to the day shift at work and had felt poorly just before she changed shifts. She was nauseated each morning and felt tired all the time. After a couple of weeks she decided to see her physician. She called the office and was able to schedule an appointment the next day. On the day of her appointment she woke up and vomited. She felt weak and dizzy but drove herself to the doctor's office anyway. She was seen immediately and was sitting in the exam room awaiting her test results when the doctor entered the room. He smiled and shook Annette's hand. "Good to see you, Annette," he said. "I know why you've been feeling sick and I can assure you it's nothing serious." Annette could usually figure out what was going on but today she didn't have a clue. "You're pregnant!" he exclaimed. Annette sat speechless. She had taken birth control pills and never expected to hear these words. "We're going to start you on prenatal vitamins and I'll give you something for the nausea which should pass in a few weeks." Annette was still speechless and just sat with her mouth open in surprise. A baby! She and Ben had talked about more children but nothing definite. Her doctor patted her on the back and said, "Congratulations!" and walks out of the room. It took Annette a few minutes to let the news sink in. She couldn't even think straight. She left the office in a state of shock. On one hand she was happy that she was pregnant and able to give Ben a child but on the other hand she was not looking forward to sleepless nights, bottles and diapers. She would have to tell Ben and the children but what would be their reaction? Annette had a lot of thinking to do.

When Ben came home from work Annette had prepared a special meal and had a quite night planned before she broke the news. As soon as Ben came home he knew something was up. Annette wasn't acting like herself and he was afraid something was terribly wrong so he didn't hesitate to question. "Annette," he said, "I know something is bothering you so let's hear it." She didn't realize he was so observant. After hesitating she blurted, "I'm pregnant!" She burst into tears. Ben was shocked for a few seconds then began to smile from ear to ear. He had always wanted a child with Annette. "That's the best news I've had in a long time!" He shouted. "Wahoo!" He grabbed Annette and hugged her so hard she could hardly breathe. Annette was happy that Ben took the news so well. They talked about the baby for about an hour. Ben was so thrilled he wanted to tell the children right away.

They called Hunter and Bethany downstairs and asked them to sit on the couch. Ben tried to be calm and explain that they both loved each of the children and wanted them to welcome a new baby but instead he blurted out, "We're going to have a baby!" Both children's mouths dropped open is astonishment. Hunter asked if it could be boy while Bethany began to frown. She couldn't believe it! If it weren't enough that Annette and Hunter took up all of her father's time but now there was going to be a baby! What if it was a boy? Bethany tried to maintain her composer but both Ben and Annette knew she disliked the idea of a baby in the house. Both children retreated back to their rooms. Bethany started hitting her pillow is anger. She was supposed to be her father's only child. How could they do this to her? She would not stand for this!

When Bethany went to visit her mother she immediately told Bell the news. Annette was pregnant. Bell was beside herself with anger. Things were getting out of hand and Bell vowed to stop the couple's progress one way or the other. They had a big fancy house, new cars, plenty of money and now of all things a baby on the way! Bell only had two run down old houses, an old car and no husband or child. Why did Annette get everything? Didn't Bell deserve to be happy too? Bell hated Annette with a passion and would spend every waking moment thinking of a plan to repay her. The only way to do this would be to involve Bethany. This way, if she were caught it would be a confused little girl who loved her father and would do anything to get him back. Yes, the perfect plan.

Annette began to feel better after the first couple of months and now that she had reached her third month of pregnancy she looked the picture of health. A glow emitted from her being as motherhood readily agreed with her. Ben was the happiest father ever. Nothing could stop him from daydreaming about his unborn child. Maybe it would be a boy! They could name him after Ben's father. If it was a girl that would be okay too! She would like just like her mother. Ben could hardly wait until the day came for his child to be born. Ben's only regret was that he had wasted so many years with Bell. If he had only met Annette years ago his life would have been so much happier.

Bell and Bethany spent the entire next visit going over their plan. It was important for Bethany to keep their secrets and not wavier when confronted. Bethany had perfected the lies and deceit with coaching from her mother. She had learned when to keep her mouth shut and how to play the poor pitiful stepchild. They would initiate the plan soon.

Annette was working upstairs in the spare bedroom making it into a nursery. She had painted clouds on the ceiling and placed borders of footballs, baseballs, and soccer balls. Yes, the baby was a boy! Ben was ecstatic. His son, named after his father, would be born in just a few months. Annette had cleaned the paintbrushes and was walking down the stairs when her foot hit something slippery. Someone had spilled an oily substance all over the steps. Annette lost her balance and tumbled down the flight of stairs hitting her head on the way down. She screamed in pain as she yelled for Hunter to call 911. Blood began to pour from Annette's loins. The bright red blood pooled underneath her as she lay in a fetal position at the foot of the stairs. Bethany came out of her room and looked down at Annette as she went in and out of consciousness. The girl smiled and slowly walked back into her room and shut the door. Hunter was terrified. He held his mother's head as the pool of blood engulfed both of them. He watched the color drain from her as he rocked back and forth while praying. Shortly the ambulance arrived and rushed Annette to the hospital. Hunter was hysterical as he called Ben.

Ben flew to the emergency room in a panic. When he arrived he found his wife lying in the bed with tubes and wires attached to her. Bags of blood were being mechanically pumped into her arm while the cardiac monitor beeped slowly in sync with her heartbeat. She looked gray in color without moving as the machines kept her body alive. Ben broke down in tears. His lovely bride was clinging to her life by a thread. How did this happen? What about the baby? The doctor walked into the room as nurses scurried around Annette. He asked Ben to step into the conference room where he sat down facing Ben. "There's no easy way to say this Ben . . ." the doctor choked back tears. "Annette lost the baby and I'm not sure she's going to make it herself. We're all praying for her." Ben felt like someone had kicked him in the stomach. His baby was dead and now he may lose the only true love he'd ever known. Ben was devastated.

He had asked the neighbor to come stay with the kids. While Hunter and Bethany were waiting for the neighbor to come over Hunter stayed in his room crying. Bethany, on the other hand was busy cleaning the bath oil that she had spilled on the stairs. No one else knew why Annette fell and her step mother didn't look very well when they wheeled her to the ambulance. Bethany softly sang to herself as she cleaned the staircase. How proud her mother would be. This had been easier than planned. Who could prove that Bethany was responsible for Annette's accident? Her father certainly will never believe otherwise. Maybe both Annette and the baby would die.

Annette was admitted to the Intensive Care Unit. Her color had improved slightly but she remained unconscious. Ben stayed by her bedside all night, praying and holding his wife's hand. By morning Annette's heart rate was normal and they finally got her blood pressure up. Annette slowly opened her eyes and saw her husband dozing in the chair beside her bed. When she moved her hand he jumped up and ran toward her. She knew by the look on his face that something was terribly wrong. He broke down crying as he gently told her what happened. Their unborn baby was dead. Annette burst into tears and the couple clung to each other sobbing. Annette couldn't remember exactly what had happened, just that she had slipped and fell down the stairs. They believed it to be a terrible accident. The loss of their child would haunt them forever but both Annette and Ben were strong and would survive this crisis.

Annette was released a week later. She couldn't bring herself to see the baby's room so Ben locked the bedroom door until they could have some time to mourn. Bethany was unusually sweet to Annette. The girl put on a show when she and Hunter discovered the news about the baby. Both Annette and Ben were surprised by her concern. Annette finally went back to work and the day to day events returned to normal.

Bell was overjoyed to hear of the accident. She just wished Annette would have died but at least the bitch was suffering from the loss of her baby. Bell was proud of her daughter. Bethany was finally taking matters into her own hands. That's the way it should be. A person had to stand up for themselves and take control of the situation. Bethany did what she had to do. The next issue on the list was Hunter. Bell had to think of some way that her daughter could get Hunter but she would have to plan this very carefully.

Annette and Ben couldn't figure out what she had slipped on. There was nothing on the stairs so did Annette stumble over her own feet? Annette said she remember slipping on the stairs. This just didn't make any sense. That is, until Hunter overheard their conversation. "Maybe it was the oil on the stairs!" he declared.

"What oil," asked Ben?

"The stairs had oil on about three or four of the steps. I saw it when I went to my room the day Mom fell."

Ben and Annette looked at each other. They hadn't cleaned anything so who did? Maybe the neighbor cleaned? Ben immediately called and asked. The neighbor said she never saw anything on the stairs when she arrived. She said she would have noticed because she immediately went upstairs when she arrived. Something sinister had happened and the couple was determined to find out what was going on. They questioned both children who adamantly denied spilling anything on the stairs.

Now that the baby was out of the way all Bell had to do is concentrate on Hunter. Although she had never met the boy but she had heard a lot of things from Bethany. According to her Hunter was a little know-it-all who got by with anything. The punishments were always harsh for Bethany but Hunter could do no wrong. "We'll see about that!" thought Bell, "that little bastard is going to suffer as well." Bell and Bethany both despised the fact that Ben had adopted Hunter.

Bell was awake until the early morning hours trying to devise her plan of action when her phone rang. It was the hospital. Ms. Emma, the wife of the elderly couple down the street had passed away. Since Bell held their power of attorney she was asked to come to the hospital and sign the appropriate paperwork. Both husband and wife had suffered from a terminal illness this was to be expected. The husband was experiencing chest pain at the loss of his wife so he was admitted. Bell got dressed and headed into town. She signed all the paperwork then preceded upstairs where she found the old man lying in a hospital bed. He didn't look well; his frail body lay motionless with the exception of slight twitching of his hands. He was ashen in color and the oxygen machine quietly pumped the life sustaining gas into his lungs. Bell sat by his side and felt his hands. They were cold to touch and slightly blue around his fingernails. "He doesn't have long," she thought. "All I have to do now is wait."

Bell had slowly skimmed money out of the couples' bank account. They currently had less than two hundred dollars left in savings while she had scammed thousands of dollars over the past few months. Bell had already planned for the old woman to be cremated because it was cheaper than having to bury her. Maybe she would take the ashes and mail them to the old woman's family. She hadn't even called them to tell them their mother was dead and that their father was critical. Maybe she would just wait until the old man died and send them both at once. Bell smiled . . . imagine the look on the family's face when they opened a package and found the ashes of their dead parents. Bell laughed to herself. There's nothing the family could do legally since Bell had the power of attorney.

Bell left for home but stopped by the couple's house first. She rummaged through their personal belongings and took any item that was of value. She found jewelry, silver, and even took food out of their refrigerator. She had no shame whatsoever. She loaded up her car and headed for home.

She had just finished unloading her car when the phone rang again. The old man was dead. The hospital staff told Bell that he was so distraught that his heart just quit. Bell couldn't have been happier. She was now the proud owner of a third home. She immediately called the funeral home to make arrangements for a second cremation. What timing! She had already made plans to help the old man meet his maker but it happened naturally. This was her lucky day!

Bell was so happy that she decided to visit Ms. Beasley, another target of hers. Bell didn't particularly care for the woman but she was loaded. Ms. Beasley's dead husband left her a small fortune as well as a huge home in the higher end neighborhood. She began trusting Bell more and more which was exactly as Bell had planned. The two women talked for a couple of hours sipping a cup of coffee. Ms. Beasley asked Bell to stay for dinner but she declined claiming she had to go to work. The truth was that Bell wanted to finalize plans for the old couple's cremation as quickly as possible.

Bell's happiness was short lived. It was time for Tim to come by to deliver his weekly check but this time he didn't have check in hand. He told Bell that he was no longer going to give her money. She had been treating him poorly and he was tired of it. Bell wasn't interested in spending any time with Tim since all she wanted was his money. He had met a lady at his new job and they had been dating for several weeks. He told Bell that it was obvious that she never really cared for him and he realized that she had been using him for quite some time. He didn't even give her time to respond as he wished her well and quickly left her standing on the porch. Bell was speechless. How dare he? Who did he think he was? She became very angry and threw her cup of coffee at his car as he pulled out of her driveway.

Ben and Annette were trying to get past losing the baby but it was hard for both of them. Maybe sometime in the future they would try again but not anytime soon. Annette firmly believed that somehow Bethany had something to do with the accident. For the second time Annette almost lost her life so she was very careful around Bethany. She didn't want to believe that a beautiful, intelligent girl could be so evil but all indications pointed to her. Bethany apparently had mastered the techniques of her mother, a woman so twisted that she didn't even know reality from fantasy. How could Annette continue to live like this? She didn't feel like she could talk to Ben about it and she understood that he loved Bethany but what would happen next? Annette felt overwhelmed. The stress of her job and family was becoming more than she could handle. Maybe she needed to see a professional . . .

Bell sat in front of a computer at the local library and logged on to a free, sleazy internet dating site. She had come up with a brilliant idea. She completed a profile for Ben: wealthy middle aged man looking for single women between the ages of eighteen and eighty, seeking kinky sexual acts, willing to spend lots of money on women looking for a good time. She gave Ben's email address along with his phone number and home address. Bell giggled out loud. "This should cause some problems!" She said to herself. "Wait until women start calling Ben for a good time!" Bell found it very humorous that she had thought of a way to cause problems for Annette and Ben and was quite proud of the idea.

Ben's phone began to ring constantly and his email was jammed full. He couldn't figure out why all these crazy women were continually calling. When he checked his email he was astounded. "What the hell is going on?" he said out loud as Annette entered the room. He saw very explicit emails from several different women who offered a variety of services. Ben immediately called the police. Annette was upset and angry. An officer arrived and took a report but informed Ben that they couldn't prove who was responsible if the IP address came from a public computer. He suggested that Ben change his phone number as well as his email address. Ben was livid. This had to be initiated by Bell. No one else could think of such a thing. He sat on the couch with his head in his hands. How much more did he and his wife have to endure? It seemed everyday presented with some type of problem. Annette sat beside her husband and sighed. They sat in silence for what seemed to be an eternity. Annette finally stood up and stated, "I love you, Ben. It doesn't matter what that piece of shit does to us she's not going to tear us apart." With that being said she left the room to start dinner. Ben felt a little better, at least his wife still believed in him. Oh how he hated his ex-wife!

The police traced the IP address to a computer in the library and quickly closed the case. Although Ben's privacy had been violated they couldn't prove who did it. They were very sympathetic to Ben's dilemma but there was nothing they could do to help. They called Ben to tell him that they were unable to obtain any proof on the person who had placed his information on the internet. Ben had changed his phone number as well as his email address but women were still showing up at their door. Annette was so frustrated that she had a fence installed around their home and placed a no trespassing sign at the gate. She just wanted to be left alone and live her life in peace. Annette had never actually hated anyone in her lifetime until now. She hated Bell, the insane, hateful woman who was doing everything in her power to destroy their happy family.

Bell received a phone call from the elderly couple's son. "I'm trying to reach a neighbor of my parents, her name is Bell." The caller stated. "This is her," Bell replied.

"I understand that my parents have passed away and you have their power of attorney. Is this correct?"

"Yes," she stated flatly

"Is there a reason you didn't contact either my sister or myself when our parents passed away?"

"No"," she again stated flatly

"Listen lady, who in the hell do you think you are tricking my parents into signing away everything they've ever worked for and then having them cremated without our knowledge? We found out through another neighbor on your street that my parents have been cremated and we didn't even know they had died! What kind of monster are you? Our attorney will be contacting you soon but I just wanted to hear it for myself that a parasite like yourself did indeed exist! Good Day!"

Bell slammed the phone into its receiver. "Let them sue!" she thought, "I've already cleared everything with my attorney. They can't touch me!" Bell was right. Her attorney had written an iron clad agreement for the couple and Bell had placed a copy in the lock box at her bank along with the cash she stole from them. She also tricked them into signing their life insurance policies over to her. Yes, it was quite the jackpot for Bell. She planned to rent their house and have a little money coming in each month and she already had a buyer for their vintage car. There was nothing their children could do about it. It would take a couple of weeks for the cremated bodies to be available for pick up so Bell would send the relatives a post card to let them know where to retrieve their parent's ashes. She had no remorse whatsoever in her actions. In fact, she was quite proud of herself.

The elderly couple's children, Sam and Diane were devastated by the death of their parents and shocked at the revelation that Bell had taken everything they owned. They hired an attorney and planned to take Bell to court. Their attorney was amazed that Bell was able to swindle their parents so easily and get by with it. They didn't know that this wasn't her first victim. Bell had perfected her skills over the past few years and was very good at fooling people. She would first appear as the pitiful, divorced spouse who had been wronged; then to make matters worse her only child was taken from her. Bell had the ability to cry at will so she would be very convincing. Some were able to see through her act but for the most part people would feel sorry for her and attempt to help her until they found out the truth.

Chapter 22

Bethany and Hunter had a very strained relationship. Hunter didn't trust Bethany and was still upset about the turtle incident. Bethany was trying hard to be kind and friendly to Hunter but he was having any part of it. He just wanted to be left alone. This infuriated his sister. She had gone out of her way to try to be nice and he was being an ass. It was important that Bethany gain his trust again in order for her and her mother's plan to work. This would take time but Bethany was sure she would succeed. After a few months Hunter spent more and more time hanging out with his sister. Maybe she wasn't so bad after all; maybe she was just having a hard time adapting to her new family. This is just what Bethany wanted. Although she hated him she had to play the game until the timing was right. The day finally came . . .

Hunter woke up early and headed downstairs to eat breakfast. Annette and Ben had already left for work since the children were old enough to stay by themselves during the day. Bethany had beaten him downstairs and had already made microwave pancakes with a big glass of orange juice. "Look Hunter, I made you breakfast!" she declared. Impressed, Hunter replied, "Hey, thanks, sis." What a thoughtful thing to do. He gobbled up the pancakes and gulped down the juice then patted Bethany on the back. "Thanks. That was great." He scurried upstairs to his room. After about thirty minutes Hunter started feeling weak. He tried to get up off his bed but almost passed out. He reached for his cell phone and called his mother. It took Annette a couple of minutes to get to the phone and she could barely hear him explain how he felt. Something deep inside Annette set off a warning. She immediately had a coworker call 911 as she stayed on the phone with him. Suddenly he stopped talking. Annette was in a panic. She screamed into the phone trying to get him to respond but to no avail. Finally, the ambulance arrived at her home. It only took a few minutes for them to place Hunter in the ambulance and head to the emergency room with sirens blasting. They couldn't revive the boy and was unable to get a blood pressure.

They EMS crew arrived shortly through the emergency room doors. Annette, along with doctors and other nurses were frantically waiting. Hunter was unresponsive and very ashen in color. They placed two IVs in his arms and hooked him up to monitors. After what seemed to be an eternity he finally opened his eyes. Annette burst into tears of happiness. Her little boy's condition had improved. The nurses and doctors breathed a sigh of relief. They began running tests on him to try to find out what had happened. To their frustration they couldn't find explanation. All the tests were negative. What could have caused Hunter's blood pressure to drop? There were no poisons or abnormalities in his lab tests, his x-rays were clear and his cardiac tests were negative. Something had to cause this but what? They would admit him overnight for observation. Annette called Ben.

Bethany was at home by herself. Annette had called and said she and Hunter would be spending the night at the hospital and her father would be home shortly after he checked on Hunter. Bethany would have her father all alone tonight and she could hardly wait. She didn't know how bad her brother's condition was but she knew her plan didn't work. Bethany had crushed one of her mother's blood pressure pills and mixed it in Hunter's orange juice. If only she had hidden his phone . . .

Ben arrived home about nine o'clock and appeared exhausted. Bethany met him at the door, crying. She was so upset about her brother that it took Ben awhile to calm her down. "Daddy, is Hunter going to be alright? I don't know what I would do if something happened to him!" she cried. Ben put his arms around his daughter to comfort her. She smiled as she hugged him around the neck. He was so easy to fool.

"Hunter's going to be just fine, baby." He said. "Now let's get you to bed. I know you've been worried."

Bethany kissed her father good night and went to bed.

Ben sat at the kitchen table with his head in his hands. Life shouldn't be this hard. It seemed every time things were getting back to normal something happens. The phone rang. It was Annette's friend who offered to come over and stay with Bethany while Ben stayed at the hospital with his wife and son. Ben gratefully accepted and took a quick shower while waiting for his wife's friend.

Bethany overheard the conversation and was furious. How could her father leave her here with someone she didn't even like only to be with Annette and Hunter? Bethany ran downstairs when she heard her father come out of the bedroom.

"Daddy, don't leave me here!" she pleaded.

"Don't be ridiculous, Bethany. You know you can't go to the hospital and Annette's friend will take good care of you." He said.

"I want to be with you!" she cried.

"Listen, I'll be back in the morning. Now go to bed." He replied firmly and shooed her upstairs to her bedroom.

Annette's friend arrived and Ben quickly left. Bethany couldn't go to sleep as she was so angry at her father. He had abandoned her for Hunter and Annette. Her mother was right. He loved them more than he loved his own flesh and blood! If only she hadn't screwed up the plan . . .

Ben arrived at Hunter's room but his son had already fallen asleep. "Hi, sweetie" he whispered to his wife. She had dozed off while sitting in a chair beside Hunter's bed. She looked up and smiled, happy to see her husband. "Did they say what happened?" he asked.

"Ben, they couldn't find anything wrong. They have no idea why his blood pressure dropped so low." She replied. "They've run all kinds of tests that came back negative."

Ben looked bewildered as he sat down on the bed and held Hunter's hand. "He's a tough little man. We'll set up appointments with a specialist and find out what's going on." He said assuring. Ben couldn't shake the disturbing feeling that something was terribly wrong. A normal healthy kid just wouldn't have become so ill this quickly. Things just didn't add up and Ben was determined to find out what happened to his son.

Hunter had slept quietly during the night with no problems. He was released the next morning to go home and follow up with his pediatrician. The following months resulted in test after test for the boy but no one was able to determine what may have happened. As far as any doctor could tell he was healthy. Bethany was so sweet and concerned during this time that no one even suspected she was the one who gave him the tainted orange juice.

Bell heard the news about Hunter from Bethany. She was proud of her daughter; Bethany had finally taken matters into her own hands and wouldn't stand for being treated badly. Bell coached her daughter every time she came to visit. They would wait awhile before they struck again for fear of being caught. Bell began to dote on her daughter. She had come to realize that the bond between mother and daughter was strong. She had taught Bethany well and as the girl grew older she became more and more like her mother. They shared something deep and dark within themselves that was constantly tugging at their sanity. Was it truly a mental illness or had they just progressed into the persons they had become? Bell lived in a fantasy world; a world that she had made in her own mind. Bethany was now becoming part of that world and sharing her mother's fantasy as well. They both enjoyed the darkness growing inside them and thrived on the feeling it gave them.

Bell continued to work a few hours a week at the nursing home. She had become friends with several of the residents and actually would spend hours after work visiting with them. They would listen intently as Bell told her sad story and offer to give Bell some of their medication to help her cope. She would even swap pills with a few of the residents and swear them to secrecy so the nursing home staff would not find out what she was up to. Bell had a pill for everything that she stashed in a large tote bag but her favorite was a medication called Xanax that she kept in her purse. She could take one of these little pills and fall asleep without the constant reminder that she had lost her family. Without the medicine Bell didn't sleep well. When she laid in her bed at night she would remember that Ben used to lay next to her while their baby slept quietly in her crib down the hall. Oh how she missed them! It just wasn't fair.

Bell awoke in a very angry mood. She had dreamed that she and Ben were back together and she once again had her family with her. When she realized that had just been a dream she became angry. It was all Annette's fault. Annette, the woman who stole her husband and daughter didn't deserve them. Why didn't Ben realize that his place was here with his wife and daughter? What kind of hold did that bitch have on him? Bell couldn't understand it and was working herself into a fury. Maybe she would go visit Ben at work; she would remind him of the good times they've had and beg him to come back home. He loved her before and could certainly love her again. That's it! She would try it.

That afternoon Bell showered and put on her sexiest dress. She didn't care that it really didn't fit well, just that her breasts spilled out of the front. She arrived at Ben's workplace just as he was leaving for the day. She approached his car just as he was getting in the driver's side. She opened the passenger door and sat down. He looked shocked as Bell pulled up her dress showing her large thighs. "What the hell do you think you're doing?" he demanded.

"Look Ben, I know you loved me once and you can love me again. We belong together. I've changed and will do anything to get you back. I love you, Ben." Bell said.

The look of surprise on Ben's face was replaced with anger. "Get out of my car and do not contact me again!" he screamed.

"Please, Ben" she begged, "We could be one big happy family again if only you would come home where you belong. If you don't want to do it for me then do it for our daughter"

Ben picked up the phone and got out of his car. "I'm calling the police! When are you going to accept the fact that I love Annette? She's the only true love I've ever known! You're insane!" he shouted.

Humiliated, Bell immediately began to cry and opened the passenger door to leave. She ran to her car sobbing loudly. She had been positive that she could make Ben see the error of his ways and come home.

Ben jumped back into his car and sped away as he called Annette.

When Ben came home Annette followed him to the bedroom to hear the details of his story. After Ben had explained what had happened Annette began to laugh. She couldn't help it; all she could picture in her mind was this large, crazy woman who thought she could lure Ben with her body. Annette fell backwards on the bed laughing hysterically. Ben didn't find the humor in it at all but at least he was happy Annette wasn't mad. Ben started to smile as he fell beside her on the bed. Tears were streaming down his wife's face she was laughing so hard. When she regained her composer she sat up and apologized to her husband. "It's pitiful, that's what it is," she said. "Who in their right mind would do such a thing?"

"It was embarrassing to me," Ben stated. "I hope no one from work saw her get in the car. I tell you, sweetie, that insane woman's getting worse and I was so mad I could have easily hit her in the face! I really should have called the police but I was so embarrassed and shocked."

Bell sobbed all the way home. She banged her fist on the dash so hard that it bloodied her knuckles. She had never been so humiliated in her entire life. She had been sure that she could change his mind; she never dreamed that he would turn her down. At one time he had promised to be with her "until death do us part." How could he be so cold and mean to someone he had once loved? Didn't he care that his own flesh and blood wanted her parents together? What kind of hold did Annette have over him? Bell was beside herself with rage. They would pay dearly for this! One way or the other Annette would suffer! Bell cried herself to sleep.

Bell fell into a deep depression. She called Bethany and claimed that she was sick and couldn't pick her up for her visit. She looked around her house and saw the repair that Ben had completed on the leaky ceiling. She looked in Bethany's room and it seemed she could smell her daughter's perfume. Bell had been in bed for two days and only got up to use the bathroom. She wanted to die. She even thought about ways she could kill herself. Maybe she could tie a rope from the ceiling fan and hang herself or possibly overdose on pills. The thought of ending the pain and frustration was comforting. She could imagine the reaction people would have when they found her cold, dead body swinging from the ceiling. Ben and Bethany would be sorry then. She searched the house for a rope. She had decided to end all of her pain and suffering. Bell stood on a chair as she firmly tied the rope to the ceiling fan then made a loop at the opposite end. She was sobbing as she put the rope around her neck thinking all the while about her husband and her precious little girl that she had lost. She couldn't live in this agony anymore. She kicked the chair hard as the loop tightened around her neck. As luck would have it she hadn't tied the loop very well so it slid up to her chin literally hanging her without killing her. A few seconds later the fan could no longer hold the excessive weight as it tore out of the ceiling. Bell fell flat on her back onto the floor and the fan hit her in her chest taking her breath away. She laid there for quite some time before she realized that she couldn't even kill herself the right way. She sobbed herself to sleep on the floor.

A friend from her support group had been calling with no answer. She was becoming worried about Bell since she hadn't been attending any meetings and had been absent from church services. Finally, the woman decided to stop by Bell's house.

She knocked on the door persistently until Bell finally swung the door open. Bell stood there with nothing on but her dirty robe that was opened in the front. Her hair was matted to the side of her head and the house emitted an odor that turned the stomach. It was obvious that she hadn't bathed in days. "Bell, what's going on? We've been worried about you!" the friend exclaimed.

"Nothing, I'm okay," replied Bell.

"No, you're not! Let me in!"

Bell was too groggy to argue from all the pills she had taken. She turned around and headed for the sofa not even bothering to try to cover her nakedness. Bell didn't care if anyone saw her like this or not. She had lost her husband and her daughter along with any hope of getting them back. Annette had taken away her hopes and dreams. Her world was crushed because of the hold that woman had on her husband.

Bell's friend called the pastor of their church who immediately came over with his wife and a few women from the church. The ladies cleaned her house and put her in the shower. They counseled with Bell for hours until she was feeling a little better. Bell loved all the attention and it actually made her feel better. The group stayed with her until the wee hours in the morning. They finally said goodnight and promised to return the next day. Bell sat on the sofa watching old movies and eating the food the ladies brought over until the sun began to stream into the windows. She was no longer suicidal; however, she was still depressed. Something had to give.

Bell agreed to seek mental counseling. She didn't have insurance so she decided to go to the local Indigent Care Facility. This medical facility only staffed mental counselors but it was better than nothing at all. She told the counselor her sad, pitiful story. The woman listened carefully to Bell and was finding it hard to believe everything that Bell was saying. It didn't make sense that the courts took her daughter away unless Bell was found unfit. When the counselor tried to question her about it Bell took offense and burst into tears. Bell began to scream at the lady and curse her. The counselor was taken by surprise and stood up trying to calm her patient but to no avail. Bell stormed out of the room and slammed the door behind her. She knew this was a mistake but thought she could actually get some help with her emotions. How dare that counselor question why Bethany had been removed from her home! She had come to the facility for help, not to be questioned about her parenting skills. Bell sped away never to return.

Chapter 23

Bethany was overly complimentary to Annette. She would smile and tell Annette how wonderful her meals were and how beautiful the house looked. Annette received so many compliments that they really didn't mean anything. Bethany seemed almost sarcastic when she said these things. It was like someone had told her to say nice things but she really had to force the words out of her mouth. Annette was still suspicious of the girl. She believed that Bethany was responsible for the empty medication bottles and Annette wondered about the oil spilled on the staircase but she just couldn't prove it. Annette was very wary around her step daughter. Bethany was a different person when her father was home. She was sweet and kind around him. Only during these times did Bethany offer to help Annette with chores and she made a point to ask to help in front of her father. When Ben wasn't around Bethany spoke very little and spent most of her time in her room.

She began to complain after a long visit with her mother that she was "fat". She would eat dinner then run up and down the road until nearly exhausted. She refused to eat anything healthy. It became the norm for Bethany to skip breakfast and lunch and only eat a small portion of her dinner. She would then exercise for hours to burn off anything she had put in her mouth. She would only drink water; nothing else. Annette would make Bethany's favorite foods but the girl refused to eat. Ben and Annette believed she purged after eating if she couldn't run or exercise and were worried about her health. She was a good twenty pounds underweight and looked sickly. Annette had to hide the bathroom scales because Bethany would check her weight several times during the day. They decided to take Bethany to see a psychiatrist. Annette set the appointment for the following week. Bethany was very angry about having to see a shrink but she was forced to go anyway.

When the doctor talked to Bethany she revealed that her mother had warned her about gaining weight. Bell had told her that she would grow up to be fat and lonely like her mother and that no man would ever want her if she were overweight. Bethany was afraid of gaining weight and took extreme measures to ensure she didn't gain even a pound. The psychiatrist spent two hours with her and determined there were several issues that needed addressing. Although she was very intelligent the doctor suggested intense therapy along with medication. She apparently was suffering from depression as well as RAD (Reactive Attachment Disorder). Bethany had been exposed of years of mental abuse from her mother and was having difficulty distinguishing right from wrong. She wasn't remorseful for anything. She always had a reason for misbehaving. Bethany never revealed the attempts on the lives of Hunter and Annette. She was very careful what she told the doctor. Bell had taught her well.

Bethany was resentful toward Annette for making her see psychiatric help. Her appointment was every Tuesday and Bethany wouldn't speak to Annette the entire trip to the doctor. When she arrived at school after her appointments she would slam the car door without saying a word. When the kids at school asked Bethany why she was absent every Tuesday morning Bethany would tell them she had a "stomach problem" and was being treated for it. The more sessions she had with the psychiatrist the clearer it was to him that this young lady had serious mental issues. He had caught Bethany in several lies and felt she had been totally dishonest with him.

It was a warm, sunny Saturday morning and Bethany didn't want to go shopping with Annette. She opted to stay at home with her father. As soon as Annette left for town Bethany came downstairs and found Ben.

"Daddy," she began, "I need to talk to you."

"What is it, Sweetie?" he replied.

"I don't want to cause any problems but Annette has been pretty mean to me lately. Ever since she lost the baby she treats me differently."

"She's been going through a lot but I'm sure she loves you very much," said Ben.

"You don't see it, Daddy. When you're here she's all nice and stuff but when you're gone she's really mean and she punishes me for things that Hunter does." Bethany was able to muster up some tears. "I try really hard to please her but she just ignores me."

Ben was surprised because he thought the two were getting along. "I'll talk with her, Honey. I'm sure she doesn't realize how hard you're trying." He kissed his daughter on her forehead and waited for his wife to return home. The more he thought about what Bethany had told him the angrier he became. Annette had been through some bad times but he didn't think she would take it out on Bethany. He suspected that deep down Annette blamed Bethany for causing her fall that resulted in the miscarriage of their baby and would never quite get over that accident.

When Annette arrived home she was busy unloading the groceries and really didn't pay too much attention to the mood her husband was in. After the final bag was carried in she sat at the counter to sip a cup of coffee. That's when she noticed something was wrong with Ben. He was too quiet and only gave her short, simple answers to her questions. When asked Ben what was wrong he told her exactly what Bethany had said.

"That's ridiculous!" exclaimed Annette, "She just trying to get sympathy from you." Annette knew somehow this day would come. She suspected that someday Bethany would accuse her of something she hadn't done and Ben would believe his daughter. Today was the day. Annette became infuriated that Ben would fall for one of Bethany's stories.

"Annette, you've been under so much stress I don't think you realize that the children are going through the loss of the baby themselves." He said quietly.

"What in God's name are you talking about?" Annette demanded.

"Ever since you lost the baby you've acted differently toward Bethany. Remember, she lost a little brother or sister as well." He replied.

"Did you ever stop and think how the oil mysteriously got on the steps and then again, mysteriously was cleaned up?" Annette was fuming and could hardly hold her composure.

"Are you blaming Bethany?" asked Ben in a not so nice tone.

Annette lost it! "Hell, yes I believe she purposely poured the oil on the steps in hopes I would fall! I also believe that she emptied all of my asthma inhalers when I needed them the most!" Annette was screaming by now and had lost all control. The truth was finally out and Annette was on a roll.

"I'll tell you something else!" she exclaimed, "I believe Bethany was responsible for putting Hunter in the hospital! I have no trust for the girl whatsoever!"

Ben just sat with his mouth open. He had never seen Annette so angry and couldn't believe his wife had just said these horrible things about his daughter. He didn't know how to respond so he stood up and quietly walked out of the room and out of the house. He got in his car and left. He was shocked. He had no idea that Annette felt this way and he had to take some time to absorb everything she had said. He trusted his wife and maybe he was just not seeing the same thing she was seeing. The more he thought about it the more sense she made; but what about Bethany? Could she really have it in her to do these terrible things? Her mother did! Ben drove around thinking for about an hour when he decided to go home. He had a lot of apologizing to do and was certainly determined to find out what part Bethany had played in the so called "accidents." Ben was torn between the love for his daughter and the truth. What if Bethany had been responsible for the loss of their unborn baby? What if she meant to kill Hunter? Maybe she really belonged in a mental hospital? Maybe he couldn't see the truth because he was her father and wanted to believe his daughter. Ben's mind was racing as he tried to decide how to handle the situation.

Annette was glad Ben left before she said something she would regret. She had said enough. She thought that maybe this was it; maybe Ben would actually believe his crazy daughter and turn on his wife. She would ready herself for the possibility. It broke her heart to think that maybe she would lose her husband but the truth was the truth and she was tired of pretending otherwise.

Ben walked in the door of their home, grabbed Annette and hugged her tightly. "I'm sorry," he said, "I know there's something wrong with Bethany and I don't blame you for it. We will work this out together and try to find the truth."

Annette was relieved. This was the Ben that she knew and loved and she realized that he really did love her.

"I love you too and yes, we will work this out together," she replied softly.

Bethany was in the kitchen when her father came home. When she saw the couple hugging she became angry. She thought that she had been clear with her father that Annette was mistreating her. He seemed sympathetic at the time so why was he hugging Annette? Something was terribly wrong. He should be mad at her! Was he going to let his wife mistreat his own daughter? How could he? Bethany was so upset that she ran to her room to cry. Her father loved his wife more than her! Oh how he would pay for this betrayal!

Bethany called her mother and explained the situation. Bell was upset when she heard that Ben had taken Annette's side. How could Ben believe his wife over his daughter? Bell tried to calm Bethany and vowed that they would devise a fool proof plan to break up the couple's relationship. She assured her she would think of something. Bethany felt a little better but was still very upset. She told her mother she loved her and hung up. She was so angry that she took a thumbtack and pulled it along her leg until she bled. Bethany repeated this again and again until the blood covered her leg. She watched as the blood trickled onto the floor and finally clotted and stopped. She smiled. It somehow made her feel less stressed to watch her own blood flow and feel the pain of the thumbtack opening into her skin. Her mother had once told her that when she becomes angry she should cause herself physical pain and it would relieve the anger. Her mother was right because the pain seemed to feed the darkness.

The next day Annette saw the cuts to Bethany's legs and asked her what had happened. Bethany told her she fell into a briar patch and scratched her legs. Although Annette did not believe her she didn't question the girl further . . . it wasn't worth the effort. She would leave it for the psychiatrist to figure out. Although Annette had many years of nursing experience she felt too close to this issue.

Chapter 24

Bell accepted her friend's invitation to attend a cookout and swim party. Her friend's brother was supposed to attend and Bell was extremely attracted to him. She found her bathing suit under the mountain of clothes piled in her closet and tried it on. It appeared a couple of sizes too small and moths had eaten a large hole in the side but Bell didn't care. She wasn't about to spend money on another one. She spent nearly an hour putting on her makeup and styling her hair. Her friend's brother was single and available and Bell intended on putting the moves on him. She tossed a worn, faded sun dress over her bathing suit and headed for the door. Bell had so much make up on that in the sunlight she actually resembled a clown.

When she arrived at the party everyone stopped talking and stared at Bell. She had removed her sundress and walked by the crowd in her swimsuit. Rolls of fat billowed from the suit and were protruding from the hole that had stretched to expose her entire side. Bell had started to sweat in the heat and her heavy makeup was running down her neck. She was looking for her friend's brother so she didn't notice the smiles or hear the whispers as she passed by. Bell carried two large bags filled with drinks and snacks. She made it almost all the way around the pool and finally settled at an empty table in which she placed her bags and sat down. She didn't see the man she had been looking for; maybe he was running late so she would patiently wait. She pulled a magazine from one of her bags and began to read ignoring the curious crowd around her.

Reggie, her friend's brother, finally arrived. Bell was ecstatic as he walked along the opposite side of the pool. He was tall, dark, and very handsome. She had met him a few years ago and he was very polite. Bell often fantasized about him; pretending they were happily married. She watched as he greeted his sister's guests. His smile was contagious and everyone had their eyes on him. He was making his way toward Bell when a thin, blonde girl called his name. He turned around and walked back to her table. He leaned over as she whispered something in his ear. He smiled and gave her a kiss on the cheek. This infuriated Bell. She had been dreaming of this man ever since she met him. She was not about to let him go this easily. Bell got up and walked toward Reggie. Just as she was close enough to touch him he turned around.

"Well hello, Reggie." She stammered.

"Hi, nice to see ya," he replied as he walked by without stopping.

Bell was undeterred. She followed him hoping to get a chance to speak with him alone. Unfortunately she was disappointed as he walked into his sister's house and before Bell could catch up with him he quickly darted out the back door and left. His sister had warned him about Bell and there was no way he was going to hang around that crazy woman.

Bell looked everywhere for Reggie and finally gave up when she overheard someone saying that he had left. Bell promptly picked up her bags and headed toward her car to go home. She was extremely disappointed and decided to take some sleeping pills and go to bed early. Maybe she could get his phone number and give him a call tomorrow. She fell asleep thinking of that handsome man at the pool.

Bell's friend refused to return her phone calls. Bell had embarrassed herself at the party and didn't even realize that she had looked like a fool. Every time she called her friend the voice mail would pick up. She had left several messages but didn't get a return call. Bell was becoming irritated. She wanted to give Reggie a call but didn't know his phone number. Her friend couldn't ignore her calls forever so she would keep trying.

Bell finally got the man's phone number and wasted no time calling him.

"Hello, Reggie?" she hurriedly asked.

"Yes," he replied.

"You probably don't remember me; my name is Bell and I'm a friend of your sister. I wanted to talk with you the other day at the pool party but you left before I got a chance to say anything. Would you be interested in having dinner with me this weekend?"

"I'm sorry, Bell, but I'm in a relationship. It's very flattering but I care for my girlfriend very much." He softly replied.

Bell was stunned and couldn't speak so she just hung up the phone. He had seemed so friendly to her and now he's saying he has a girlfriend? She was sure there was some kind of spark when they met at the pool party. "Damn!" said Bell aloud. She was disappointed as she had plans to date this man. Bell sat on the couch. "It's because I'm over weight!" she thought. "What man would want to go out with a fat hog?" She fell into a state of depression and self pity once again.

Bell didn't even bother to go to work at the nursing home the next day; all she did there was cafeteria work. She lay in bed until noon when she finally got up to fix something to eat. She missed Ben and Bethany. Why did they choose to leave her? She had been a decent wife and mother. Annette just had their minds twisted and they didn't realize how good they had it here at home. Annette . . . oh how Bell hated her. She would do anything to get rid of that woman! If she had the chance she would blow that bitch's head off!

Annette was becoming more and more stressed by Bethany's behavior. Until just a few months ago she could at least hold a conversation with the girl but not anymore. Bethany would either ignore her or rattle off something that made no sense what so ever. At times it was like talking to a five year old child. She would jump from one topic to another all within the same breath. Bethany would walk through the other rooms just to avoid seeing Annette. When they went shopping the girl would walk several steps behind her step mother as if ashamed to be seen with her. This annoyed Annette to no end.

Ben received a phone call from the kid's school. The math teacher asked Ben if he could come alone for a meeting regarding Bethany. Ben agreed to stop by on his way home. When he arrived at the school he was ushered to the teacher's classroom. She asked him to have a seat and proceeded to tell him what she had been told by Bethany "in confidence."

"I'm not trying to get in your business but I have to follow up anytime a child comes to me with a problem. Your daughter had told me in detail that she is being abused by her step mother. Although I will have to report this to the authorities I wanted to speak with you first." She said.

Ben couldn't believe his ears. "What sort of things are you talking about?" he asked.

"She told me that her step mother cooks dinner then sits down to eat in front of her, not allowing her to eat. She also stated that she is denied medication when she's sick and that she is made to clean up after her step brother. Additionally, Bethany tells me that she is punished severely whenever she does anything wrong."

Ben smiled. "I'll tell you what, go ahead and contact whoever you want but everything you've just told me is a blatant lie. Bethany has some serious mental issues and is looking to stir up trouble whenever possible."

The teacher seemed surprised. "She's very convincing, Sir."

"I'm sure she is; she learned this directly from her insane mother. Anything my daughter tells you is more than likely a figment of her imagination. I know you're just trying to do your job but this conversation is over. Thank you for your concern," stated Ben as he walked out the door. He had started to become very angry at his daughter.

By the time Ben had arrived home he was livid and ready to confront Bethany but she had already been picked up by her mother for her visit. Ben explained to Annette what the school counselor had told him. Annette was hurt and angry and suggested they go to the school and speak directly with the counselor. Ben agreed, however, it would have to wait until Monday when school was back in session.

Bethany told Bell all about speaking to the counselor. She was quite proud of the fact that Annette may get into trouble. If Annette went to jail then she would have her father all to herself. Bell told her daughter how proud she was of her standing up for herself and not putting up with Annette's abuse. "Bethany, if you keep trying sooner or later Annette will grow tired of all the drama and leave your father," said Bell, "You've come so close and I think this time someone will believe you." When they arrived at Bell's house there was a letter in the mailbox waiting for her. The letter was from Annette. It read:

Bell,

Bethany and I went to see her psychiatrist and he advised Ben and I have a talk with you. Since I know this would be impossible I am writing this letter. You obviously have been saying some things about me and Hunter to Bethany.

I couldn't care less what you have to say about me but you are causing great harm to your daughter. She loves you and believes the nasty things you are saying even though you don't even know me or Hunter well enough to have an opinion. You need to know that no matter what you do or what you say will not change the fact that Ben and I are together. Trying to get Bethany to break us up will <u>not</u> work! I did not "steal" him away from you nor did I "steal" your child from you. They left you on their own free will after years of mental abuse. Telling Bethany differently is only causing harm to her.

If you care at all for your daughter then you need to cease this behavior immediately. You claim to be a Christian woman but indeed you are just hiding behind your religion. Bethany has enough problems without you creating more for her. When you tell her things like "You're going to grow up and be fat and lonely like me" you are damaging the girl. Ben did not leave you because you're overweight; he left you because you were hateful and mean to him.

You tell Bethany that you are so poor and can't afford anything for them when in reality if you were to work a full time job not only would you be able to buy her something other than used clothing that is too large for her, but I believe you would feel better about yourself as well. Stop the self pity, Bell; this isn't good for your daughter. She feels sorry for you and feels badly when you try to make it all MY fault. You have blamed me for all of your problems when in reality I have nothing to do with your situation.

Finally, you have done everything in your power to cause us problems. I have documented proof that not only have you forged Ben's name, you have used our insurance for your own, you opened credit cards in Ben's name and you took out insurance on your home in my husband's name. I have had enough of your bizarre behavior and it will no longer be tolerated. You have the option to stop now or suffer the legal consequences of your actions.

Bethany is no longer a child. She is a young adult and will soon be moving away to fulfill her dreams. Don't take that away from her with your jealousy and revenge toward me and my husband. You have lost custody of your child so why don't you try to make what little time she spends with you enjoyable instead of trying to cause trouble for her? As she grows older she will eventually see you for what you are and you will truly be alone.

Annette

Bell read the letter twice then blew up. "How dare that uppity bitch say these things to me?" she thought, "Who in the hell does she think she is? Bell had done everything in her power to get rid of Annette but just couldn't succeed. What did she have to do to accomplish this? Bethany would have to be more persistent and help her rid herself of her wicked step mother. Bell would get her husband and child back if it was the last thing she ever did!

The weekend flew by and Bethany didn't want to go home. She wanted to stay with her mother. "You have to go, Bethany, or otherwise your father and Annette will have me put in jail." Bell really didn't want Bethany to live with her; she had enjoyed not having to take care of a child. It was nice to see her every other weekend but every day was too much. "Besides, you know I've been sick and unable to care for you properly." Bell took Bethany home.

A knock on the door awakened Bell the next morning. It was the Department of Children's and Family Services . . . again. She slowly walked to the door and opened it. The young lady at the door introduced herself and said she needed to talk with Bell. Although Bell was hesitant about talking to DEFAC she ushered the young woman inside. Ms. Culpepper, the woman, reluctantly sat on the worn, tattered sofa. She began her conversation with Bell on a positive note. "I know how hard it is being a single mother," the lady began, "but we have a complaint filed against you about the condition of your home."

"What?" asked Bell.

"The complaint stated that you are allowing your daughter to visit at your home and they say that's it is endangering her health," Ms. Culpepper stated calmly.

"My house is clean!" demanded Bell.

"Do you mind if I look around?" the lady asked.

"I guess that would be okay," said Bell hesitantly.

Ms. Culpepper walked into the kitchen where dishes were piled up to the window. Cockroaches scattered everywhere as soon as she turned on the light. There wasn't any food to eat in the refrigerator and the cabinets were empty with the exception of a few crackers. The lady was constantly writing something in her book. Bell said, "I haven't had a chance to go grocery shopping yet."

The lady paused and briefly looked at Bell then continued from room to room. When she arrived in Bell's bedroom the odor was almost too much. Clothes were piled high in the master bedroom closet and boxes of unknown items were stacked to the ceiling. There was fecal matter from Bell's dog she had over a year ago that had dried and still remained in the carpet. Pill bottles were stacked on her bedside table along with plates of dried, half eaten food. The stench was overwhelming as Ms. Culpepper made her way through the bedroom to the bathroom. The toilet looked like it hadn't been flushed in several days and the sink was black from mildew.

She moved to Bethany's bedroom where she immediately noticed the unmade bed with white sheets that were so filthy they looked brown. Clothes were strewn about the room with rat droppings covering the clothes. The closet was so full of junk that Ms. Culpepper was afraid to completely open the door for fear that everything would come tumbling out. The room smelled horrible.

The lady had seen enough. She gingerly sat down again on the sofa and explained the situation to Bell. "From what I've seen today, Bell, this house should be condemned. You are going to have to clean this place before we can allow your daughter to visit. This is a health hazard and needs to be rectified immediately. I'm surprised you're not sick from all this filth." She said.

Bell began to cry. "I've have been sick and unable able to clean. I don't know who reported this but if they knew me they would know that my house usually isn't this dirty. I haven't been the same since my husband ran off with another woman then took my only child away from me."

"Bell; there are dog feces in your bedroom carpet!" Ms. Culpepper explained. "I really have no choice but to put you on notice. When you've cleaned this place then give me a call and I'll re-evaluate the situation." The woman didn't want to hear Bell's tale of woe. She then got up and walked out of the house before the stench made her vomit.

Bell's was beside herself with anger. Who could have called the Department of Children's and Family Services? It had to be Annette. No one else would do this. Bell didn't know she could hate Annette any more than she already did but it was true, she hated her even more. She reveled in the thought of buying a gun and blowing Annette to pieces. Or maybe she would get a chance to run over her with a car. That would be sweet! She would talk with Bethany. The girl is going to have to help in getting rid of Annette.

Bell grudgingly called a cleaning service to clean her home. They charged her nine hundred dollars to get the house back into a livable condition. Ms. Culpepper came by for a second inspection and told Bell she would once again allow Bethany to visit but Bell would have to keep the home clean. She would come back in sixty days for another inspection.

Ben and Annette went to school to meet with the counselor. They explained the situation to her and assured her that Bethany was just making accusations about Annette. They told her about Bethany's mental condition as well as Bell's. The counselor smiled and nodded but the couple was sure that she didn't believe them. Before they left the school Ben urged the counselor to call the police if she had any doubts and then wished her good day. It was clear that Bethany had learned very well from her mother on how to gain sympathy and how to lie at will.

Bethany was becoming quite defiant toward Annette. Whenever Annette told her to do something the girl would completely ignore her and continue doing whatever she wanted. Although she would get punished for her actions she didn't care. Annette was not her mother and she didn't have to listen to her. The fact of the matter was she hated her step mother almost as much as Bell hated her. Bethany wasn't gaining any weight and was extremely underweight for her age group. She still complained about being "fat". She refused to eat breakfast and lunch and only ate a small portion of dinner. She would drink only water. Bethany had become so underweight that her menstrual periods stopped completely. Ben and Annette were becoming very concerned about her health.

When Annette informed that doctor of Bethany's obsession with her weight he suggested changing her medication along with therapy. This didn't seem to help; in fact Bethany's condition was gradually worsening. She would hold conversations with herself and continue self mutilation whenever she could. Her actions placed a huge strain on the family. Bell encouraged this behavior and even went so far to tell Bethany how to hurt herself without being detected. For example, she could cut her legs as long as she wore pants to cover up the wounds. Bethany would even pull handfuls of hair out of her scalp until the blood ran down her face. She would stand in front of a mirror and smile as the warm blood dropped onto the floor. She would then run downstairs and tell Ben that Hunter pulled her hair. Ben never punished Hunter because he didn't believe his daughter. He would just tell them both to get along. He was tired of all the drama and it was slowly wearing him down.

The drama had taken a toll on Annette as well. She developed problems sleeping and was feeling stressed all the time. She wasn't eating normally and was tired most of the time. Before they were awarded custody of Bethany Annette was sure that they would become one big, happy family. She had no idea of the turmoil that she and Ben would have to endure. She loved Bethany on some level but knowing in her heart that the girl had tried to kill both her and Hunter she was having a hard time keeping positive thoughts and feelings about her. Annette just wanted to strangle the girl at times; especially when Bethany would go to Ben and play her "poor pitiful me" role. Ben would always fall for it which annoyed Annette tremendously.

Chapter 25

School was out for the summer so Bethany went to visit her mother for the entire week. They were both excited and had made plans to go to several places, just two wild and crazy girls having fun. Bell would have plenty of time to discuss ways to get rid of Annette. If they put both of their heads together surely one of them could come up with something worthwhile.

Bethany waited outside the home for her mother to pick her up. She started jumping up and down when she saw Bell's car pull into the driveway. She missed her mother terribly but she really liked the fancy house and swimming pool at her dad's. Annette would buy her new clothes frequently (something her mother never did for her) and she had plenty of food to eat. If only it was her mom instead of Annette who lived here, life would be perfect. There had to be a way to get Annette to leave.

Bell pulled into the driveway and made a u-turn on the freshly planted grass in the front yard. Bethany jumped in and Bell spun tires in the fresh dirt, laughing at the thought of how angry Ben and Annette will be when they see tire tracks on their new lawn. Annette saw everything from the kitchen window and if she could have gotten her hands on Bell she would have beaten her senseless. It was obvious that she did this on purpose. This type of behavior was typical for Bell; anything she could do to aggravate the couple made her very happy. Bethany laughed along with Bell as they discussed how long it would take to repair the lawn.

Bell had planned a big weekend for the two of them. They would go to the free concert in town and then to the church for a free meal. It was homecoming for the church and they always served an enormous amount of food for the congregation. Bell wouldn't have to spend a dime. She wanted her daughter to meet a man named Frank that she had been seeing for a couple of weeks. He was quite a bit older and not very sophisticated but at least he cared about her. He believed everything she told him and would do anything she asked of him. All she had to do was spend a night or two per month with him and he was happy. He didn't have much money but his father was quite wealthy. Bell would go with him to his father's house and she would clean and do small chores for him. He was always very grateful for the help and would slip Bell a hundred dollar bill whenever her friend wasn't looking. She told the old man that his son would be upset if she took money from him so he was careful to hand her the money while Frank was busy. The old man even bought her a cell phone so he could call when he needed something. She never mentioned this to Frank.

While Bethany was gone to visit her mother Annette was upstairs collecting dirty clothes in Hunter and Bethany's room. She noticed in the girl's room a notebook at the bottom of the clothes hamper. She started to thumb through it when a picture caught her eye. Bethany had drawn a picture of a woman lying in bed and a girl standing over her with a knife. Blood was dripping from the end of the knife as well as covering the woman lying in the bed. The picture took Annette by surprise. The words written beneath the picture read, "Goodbye Annette." She continued to look at the rest of the pictures and was shocked. Page after page showed drawings of a girl killing a woman in various ways. One was a gun in the woman's mouth with brains scattered on the wall, another was a woman cut into pieces with an ax, and still another showed a woman falling down stairs lying in a puddle of blood. The final page had large words that read, "KILL ANNETTE!"

Annette's legs felt weak and she had to sit down on the bed. How could a child hate her this much? What exactly was wrong with her step daughter? She knew the girl hated her but to draw pictures of herself killing was a grave concern. Was Bethany a psychopath? She hurried downstairs to show Ben. When he saw the pictures he too was concerned but wasn't as upset as Annette. "It's probably her way of expressing her emotions." He said. "I would be more worried if she held all her anger inside."

"Are you insane?" she blurted.

"Think about Annette, yes she's been hateful to you and I know she doesn't like you but she's never raised a hand to hurt you. It's just her childish way to feel like she's getting even with you."

Annette couldn't believe he was not taking this as a serious sign that his daughter was dangerous. She didn't want to argue but she would never go to sleep without her bedroom door locked. Additionally, she would mention this to Bethany's psychiatrist. This girl had deep seated issues and Annette didn't know what to do about them. The whole thing was unnerving. Annette felt alone and afraid of what Bethany was actually capable of doing. She loved Ben and knew this was his only child but it couldn't be any clearer that the girl was demented. Maybe she was analyzing things too much, reading something else into the situation that wasn't really there. Annette thought that maybe she, herself should talk with someone professionally. No! She was right and she knew it! She hadn't just imagined the oil on the steps or the mysterious drop in Hunter's blood pressure. She was sure that Bethany had something to do with all of it and Ben just couldn't see the truth because that was his daughter.

Annette made an appointment with Bethany's psychiatrist for the end of the week. She would go see him before Bethany came back from her mother's house. Something was terribly wrong and she didn't know what to do about it. She had to talk to someone since she couldn't talk to Ben about it.

The end of the week came and Annette found herself in the doctor's office. She explained in detail the situation and expressed her fears. The psychiatrist was silent for a few moments taking in all that had been said.

"This is very complicated since nothing has been proven. If what you say if true, however, I believe that Bethany needs to be hospitalized for awhile for observation and evaluation. It's difficult to determine what's going on with her when I only see her once a week. It's obvious that she has some deep seated issues but I can't diagnose her without extensive testing. Would your husband agree to this?"

"I'm not sure," Annette replied, "Let me speak with him. I'm sure he wants what's best for Bethany."

"Very well then," he said, "give me a call tomorrow and let me know your decision once you've had a chance to talk with her father."

Annette thanked him and walked to her car. How should she approach Ben about this matter? Was he going to blow up? She would have to choose the right time to approach her husband.

Bell and Bethany was having a great time together. The two of them seem to have bonded their relationship. While driving by the park they noticed a man parked in the parking lot with a cage full of puppies. "Look, Mom!" shouted Bethany, "Free puppies!"

Bell pulled into the parking lot so they could see the animals. There were six tiny balls of fur in a cage each one light brown in color. Bethany had always wanted a dog of her own. Bell was feeling quite generous and decided to let her daughter take her pick. Bethany chose the runt. She held the puppy close as it snuggled into her neck as they drove to Bell's house. Each time Bell glanced at the puppy the dark feelings inside her began to manifest. Oh the fun she would have with the puppy once Bethany goes back home. They stopped by the pet shop to buy food and a kennel for the dog. Bell would allow the dog inside while her daughter was there but the animal would live in a small crate under the porch as soon as Bethany was gone. (Of course she didn't tell her daughter this.)

Bethany played with her new pet all day and let him sleep with her at night. The next morning no one took the dog outside to take care of his business so he defecated in the floor. Bell refused to clean it so she threw a towel over the feces. It would dry sooner or later and she could vacuum it up. This continued throughout the week and by the weekend her house smelled horrible.

Annette fixed Ben his favorite meal before she approached him about Bethany's situation. After dinner she sat down with him and explained in detail what the doctor had said. Ben sat quietly and listened intently as his wife spoke. Although he didn't want to admit it he knew something was wrong with his daughter. He also was convinced that they needed to do something to help her but he wasn't sure exactly what that was. Finally Ben agreed that he would consider in patient treatment for Bethany, however, he wanted to get a second doctor's opinion. Annette grudgingly agreed. She would make the appointment tomorrow.

Bethany arrived home an hour late. She wanted to bring home her puppy but knew neither her father nor Annette would allow it. Bell promised to take good care of the dog while Bethany was away. When Bell arrived home she took the puppy's crate and placed it under the staircase of the front porch. She slung the little dog into the crate and slammed the door shut. It was raining heavily and Bell had built her house in a flood zone. Water continued to creep into the crate as the puppy whimpered throughout the night. By morning the dog was standing in cold water up to its belly. The animal was shivering when Bell left to go to work at the nursing home. She kicked the crate and scolded the puppy, "Shut up!" The poor miserable animal was left with no food or water for the rest of the day.

When Bell arrived home the water had somewhat receded but the dog was still wet. She opened the crate and lifted the helpless puppy into the air. "Are you hungry?" she asked. She took the dog inside and dried it with a towel. She opened a can of dog food but didn't feed him right away. She was going to have some fun. She held a morsel in her hand and when the puppy tried to eat it she would slap him hard across the face until he yelped. She then lowered her hand as if to let him eat food and repeated the abuse. The dog was starving so it continued taking the abuse until she finally allowed it to take a bite. Bell continued this until the food was gone. She was amazed at how many times the dog returned to eat after being slapped so hard. He must have been really hungry. She smiled and felt the warmth of darkness well up inside her.

After the puppy was full he laid on the rug in front of the sofa. Bell called him to her and petted him, rubbing his fat little belly. He was actually very cute. His soft, brown fur had dried and he was finally content. Bell found a thick string and tied its rear legs together and watched while the animal struggled to walk. She thought it funny how he dragged his back legs around the room. She soon tired of it and set the puppy free. Suddenly, she had a thought; she snatched up the puppy and folded one of its back legs forward against its abdomen. She then took the string and wrapped it around the dog's body and leg so that the leg was tight against its body. Now she had a three legged dog. She sat the puppy down and laughed as it attempted to walk and then fell. The puppy yelped in pain as he tried time and time again to walk. This too did not hold Bell's interest very long. She didn't get the satisfaction as before when she tortured an animal so she once again freed the dog. She was getting tired so she tossed the puppy into its crate outside.

The neighbors around Bell had seen the puppy in the crate with no food or water. One day, after a heavy rain the night before, one of the neighbors had seen enough and called the local police department about the neglected animal. When the police arrived Bell wasn't home. They contacted animal control who took the puppy away. Bell returned home to find a notice on her door to contact the police officer. She called and found that she had been cited for animal neglect. She broke down and cried stating she didn't know what else to do with the dog that her daughter had brought home. She lied and said the girl had planned to take the dog home with her but her step mother changed her mind and wouldn't allow it. Bell would have to pay a large fine and would not be allowed to keep the puppy. She was advised not to replace the puppy and was also told what would happen if she committed this crime again.

Bell was livid. She had plans for that dog and now she had to pay a lot of money to stay out of jail. She just wished the damn neighbors would mind their own business! What had she ever done to them in order for them to turn on her and call the police? Bell stood outside on her porch and glared at the people living next door. She held her middle finger high in the air then turned quickly and slammed her front door hard, cursing at the neighbors.

Annette couldn't get an appointment for Bethany for another month. Unfortunately, they would have to wait until then to get a second opinion. They planned to wait until the day before her appointment before they told her the news. There wasn't any reason to upset the girl now.

Bethany was unusually complimentary to Annette. She was overly friendly, so much that Annette became suspicious about her motive. Maybe she wanted something or wanted Annette to do something for her since that was the only time Bethany was nice to her step mother. Bethany talked about her new puppy and how much she loved it. She even thought up a name, Roscoe. She told Annette how the dog slept with her and how he could sit when told, going on and on about the puppy. When she finally called her mother she immediately asked about the dog. Annette heard a shrill scream as Bethany dropped the phone and ran upstairs yelling and crying. Bell had told her that someone stole the puppy. Bethany was devastated.

She stayed in her room for days only showing her face to eat a little something. She wouldn't bathe until Ben intervened and forced her to. She didn't want to talk with anyone nor did she want to listen to anyone. Both Ben and Annette tried to reason with her but to no avail. She would have to work things out on her own but they were very worried about her mental health. Hunter tried to get her to play video games with him but she screamed for him to get out of her room. It would take some time for Bethany to get over the loss of her pet.

Hunter had received a tiny mouse for his birthday and played with the tiny creature every day. He took great care of the animal and ensured it had plenty of food and fresh water. Bethany hated the mouse. Not only was she jealous that Hunter had a pet but she hated mice. There had been so many at her mother's home that she despised the little rodents. Bethany would patiently wait until Hunter was outside playing and she would sneak into his room and violently shake the tiny mouse's cage. She would poke at the creature with pencils until it squealed. She took great delight in torturing the animal. Hunter noticed that the cage was in disarray but had no idea what his sister was doing.

Chapter 26

Bell woke up feeling great. She had just heard from her attorney regarding the old couple she had scammed. She had an airtight case and the couple's children couldn't touch her. She had plenty of money and three houses so now she could spend her time thinking of ways to aggravate her ex-husband and his wife. She had called both of their places of employment to complain about them but she wasn't taken seriously. She had even called the police department to claim they were selling drugs but they too didn't believe her. What could she do? There had to something that would put a strain on Ben and Annette. She decided to search the internet to see if she could come up with something new."

Bell logged on to every sleazy website she could find and entered Annette's name and phone number. She made up information on dating sites stating that Annette was looking for "a good time" and was available for just about anything and everything. Bell smiled to herself; "Just think of the calls Annette will be receiving soon!" she thought. Bell continued throughout the day while placing Annette's information on hundreds of websites. Annette's phone began to ring. She was receiving emails faster than she could delete them. Men from all over the world were contacting her and emailing very explicit messages and pictures as well. This same thing had happened to Ben so Annette was sure that Bell had something to do with it but how could she prove it? Bell was smart enough not to use her own computer. She had sat at the library all day so she couldn't be traced. Annette became frustrated in a very short period of time and called the phone company to have her number changed. Now she would have to contact everyone she knew to give them her new number. What a pain! When would Bell leave her alone?

The next morning Bell had an idea. If she could just hire someone that was smart enough and pretty enough to convince Annette that she was Ben's girlfriend that certainly would ruin the couples' relationship. Bell contacted everyone she knew that might be able to help her. She finally came up with one of the local strippers named Sheila. She explained in detail what needed to be done and Sheila agreed for a large sum of money. Ben would work out at the gym every Monday, Wednesday, and Friday evening and Sheila would be there to make friends with him. What a perfect idea! If Sheila could pull this off it would be well work the money.

The following Monday, true to her word, Sheila was at the gym when Ben arrived. He started on the treadmill so Sheila followed and picked the equipment beside him. She was a stunning young lady with a golden tan and scantily dressed. She started a conversation with Ben but he gave her very little attention. She was persistent each day he was at the gym for several months. She didn't push the friendship at first but one day she "accidently" slipped and fell on the treadmill. Ben rushed to her aid just as he would have anyone that needed assistance. She put her arms around his neck as he carried her to the front office for evaluation. She was extremely thankful and gave him her number. Ben didn't think too much about it and stuck her phone number in the pocket of his gym shorts. He just thought she was a nice, young lady. Ben was friendly to her but wasn't attracted to her at all. She, on the other hand was blatant about her intentions. She had grown very fond of Ben. Bell had hired a private investigator to take pictures of Ben and Sheila on various days for a three month period. Some of the pictures appeared that the two of them were leaving the gym together. That's all Bell needed.

The day came when Sheila would present the evidence to Annette. She called Annette and told her she was a friend of Bens and would like to meet with her to discuss something very important. Normally, Annette would have just hung up but something told her to meet this lady. Sheila was the name of the piece of paper Annette had found in Ben's gym shorts. She didn't think too much of it at the time but she had kept the phone number which was the same number that this woman was calling from. They agreed to meet at the local coffee shop when Annette got off from work. When Annette entered the shop she saw a very tanned, blond young woman sitting at one of the booths. "Sheila?" she asked.

"Yes," the young woman replied extending her hand, "thank you for coming."

Annette sat down on the opposite side of the table. Sheila began by saying that she had thought things through before she had decided to call Annette.

"I just couldn't take it anymore. I have been feeling so guilty when I found out Ben was married." She stated flatly. "We have been having an affair." Sheila pulled the pictures out of the envelope and spread them across the table. Although they didn't show anything intimate there were several that could be construed as the two of them being together.

"I'm very sorry," she lied, "I didn't know he was married."

Annette felt sick to her stomach. Her husband whom she trusted completely was clearly involved with this woman although he had never mentioned her whatsoever. She could not believe this was happening; it felt like a dream and she would wake up any moment. There had to be an explanation but the pictures didn't lie. It looked like Sheila and her husband was leaving the gym together. There were pictures of Sheila leaning over Ben's car showing a lot of cleavage. Why would he do this? Annette knew that had some problems but why would he have an affair? Maybe he was unhappy and just wouldn't discuss it. Maybe he was going through a midlife crisis. Annette felt dizzy and weak. She just sat there staring at the photos.

"I don't know what to say," Said Annette, "I'm shocked!"

"I know this is a surprise for you and I'm very, very sorry," said Sheila, "I thought you needed to know." She got up and left Annette sitting in the booth with the photos spread out on the table.

Annette couldn't move. It was just too much for her to comprehend. Her loving husband apparently had betrayed her. What was she supposed to do now? Tears streamed down Annette's face as she gathered the photos and placed them in the envelope. She left a twenty dollar bill on the table to cover Sheila's drink and quickly left the building. She ran to her car and sat behind the steering wheel for at least an hour trying to process everything she had just heard. She headed home.

Ben had just arrived home from work when he heard Annette's care in the driveway. She must have had to work late. He missed his wife when they were apart so he was happy to see her walk through the door . . . but something was wrong. She had been crying and seemed very angry. She didn't say anything at all and walked directly into the bedroom as Ben followed.

"Honey, what's wrong?" he asked.

Annette couldn't even speak as she handed him the photos. He opened the envelope and looked at each picture with disbelief. This was the girl from the gym but the pictures appeared as if the girl was with him. He had been friendly to her but nothing even close to what the pictures implied.

"Annette, these are not what you think," he said. "I recognize this girl but I was never with her."

"What am I supposed to think, Ben? I found her phone number in your pocket!"

"Look, I know this looks bad and I don't know what's going on but I intend to get to the bottom of this!" Ben was near panic. Someone had set him up! "Give me the phone number, Annette, I'm going to call this woman right now!" Ben was angry. Someone was trying to ruin his marriage and he was determined to find out who and why.

Annette, still not believing her husband reached in her purse and handed Ben Sheila's phone number. He immediately dialed the number then quickly hung up. He had an idea.

"Honey, call her and tell her you need to meet her one more time. I want you to meet with her and I will show up so we can confront this bitch together!"

Annette had never seen her husband this angry. Maybe he was telling the truth. It would certainly expose the truth if she and Ben confronted Sheila so she agreed. Annette called her and told her that she wanted to meet again one final time before she left Ben. Sheila agreed for the next afternoon at the same coffee shop.

Annette arrived a few minutes after Sheila then signaled her husband that the meeting was taking place. Ben walked through the door and headed to their table.

"My wife and I would like to know just who you are and why you're trying to break up our marriage!" he firmly stated, "and we're not leaving until you come clean!" Ben sat down beside her blocking her exit. He was so furious that Sheila became frightened.

"Look, I'll tell you everything! I've already got my money from the lady that hired me so I don't give a damn and I don't need any trouble." She said, "It was your ex-wife. It was her idea and she paid me a lot of money to ruin your marriage." Sheila explained Bell's idea and the instructions she had been given by her.

Annette's body was shaking from the rage. Everyone has breaking points and this was Annette's. She lunged across the table at Sheila and swung her fist hitting the woman square in the face. Blood instantly poured out Sheila's nose as her eyes filled with tears. Sheila grabbed her face and bolted over her chair to get away. She ran out of the building as if it were on fire.

Ben stared at his wife. He had never seen her out of control like this. The fact of the matter was, Annette had never hit anyone in her life. She didn't know what had come over her; it was like she wasn't in control of her own actions. They both sat there for awhile thinking that Sheila had called the police by now but no one responded. Ben and Annette finally left and walked to their car both still in the state of shock not saying a word to each other. Although Annette was ashamed of her primitive behavior she felt quite good after letting go of her anger. Ben was astounded that his loving, gentle wife acted so violently when her marriage was threatened. Somehow, this made her even more endearing to him. They drove home silently.

Sheila had run to her car with blood dripping from her nose. She didn't think it was broken but it hurt like hell. She would have called the police but she had a bag of marijuana in her purse so she opted not to call. Sheila finally got the bleeding stopped but both of her eyes were starting to turn black. Bell owed her more money after this smack in the face. She would call her later; right now all she wanted to do is get home and lie down. She would never mess with that couple again!

When Bell heard that things went poorly she was livid. This had been the perfect plan; there had been many hours of thought and planning but she had underestimated Ben and Annette. If things had gone as planned Annette would be filing for a divorce and Ben would soon be free. This stupid little tramp had to go and run her mouth and tell everything to them. Bell still owed her two thousand dollars but she was not about to pay her now that she spilled the beans! That certainly was not part of the plan. This had been Bell's ultimate scenario but now it was ruined.

When Ben and Annette returned home neither of them spoke of the incident. They went about their evening as if nothing had happened; never to be mentioned again.

Annette never discussed the attack but she thought about it often. It worried her that she had acted in such a manner. She had dedicated her life as a caregiver; rendering aid to the sick and injured, relieving pain and caring for others. She always believed that everyone had something good inside them regardless how bad they seemed on the outside. Now she, herself, had injured another person. What happened? Had she released a darkness inside of her that lay dormant all these years? Does every living person have an evil deep down inside that rears its ugly head when provoked? This worried Annette and she didn't think she would ever be the same again. Would she be able to control this monster? How would this attack affect her? Annette didn't dare discuss this even with her best friend.

Hunter was watching his favorite movie when Bethany entered the room and wanted to borrow his CD. He was annoyed at the intrusion and after saying "no" demanded she leave his room. This angered his sister. She stomped her foot as she left and screamed that she hated him as she slammed his door. After the movie ended Hunter went outside to take a walk in the woods. When he returned he heard his mouse squealing softly. When he looked in its cage he saw his beloved pet lying on its side bleeding. It had an incision-like cut the length of its belly while entrails spilled outside of its body. The little creature was barely alive and was quivering. Hunter watched the tiny creature as it took one last breath. He was traumatized. He screamed for his mother as he sat beside the cage and cried. Annette heard his scream and ran upstairs. She was horrified when she saw the little mouse then anger followed. Not just normal anger but the kind that wells up inside and explode outward.

Annette immediately stormed into Bethany's room where she sat on her bed watching television. Annette grabbed her by the arm and demanded, "What the hell have you done?"

Bethany tried to act surprised but she smiled at Annette and responded, "Nothing, why?"

"You know why!" screamed Annette, "Why would you do something like that to a helpless creature?"

"You're hurting me!" stated Bethany.

"You are a sick, demented girl! I should beat your ass!" Annette was nearly out of control . . . again . . . so she let go of Bethany's arm and stormed out of the room to comfort Hunter.

Hunter was curled up on his bed, sobbing loudly. Annette knew there was nothing she could say to make him feel better. She retrieved a small box and gently laid the dead animal inside. They would have a funeral for the little mouse and at least get Hunter some kind of closure.

"We'll bury him, Hunter." She said softly as she gently rubbed his shoulder. "Let's take him outside to the garden and give your pet a proper burial."

Hunter nodded his head, still crying softly. Annette and Hunter went outside by the flower garden and buried the tiny pet. They placed flowers on the animal's grave. Annette felt sorry for her son and worried that next time it may not be a pet that suffered. After the ceremony Hunter went to his room to mourn. Annette called Ben. When he arrived home he and Annette decided that they would take Bethany to the Mental Hospital first thing in the morning. "I really should have done this earlier, Annette, but I was blind to the fact that my own flesh and blood could be so cruel. I'm sorry, honey, Bethany needs help and I should have institutionalized her years ago."

The next day Annette sent Hunter to her friend's house to spend the day with her son. They called Bethany downstairs to let her know their decision. They explained in detail what she could expect and what they expected from her. They sent her to her room to pack and get ready to go to the hospital. Bethany ranted and raved all the while sobbing loudly. She didn't want to go to any hospital and she loudly screamed that she "wasn't crazy." It was harder for Ben that it was for Annette to force Bethany into a mental institution but he knew it was their only alternative. She needed help and this was the only place that could give her the help she needed. The finally got Bethany into the car and the three of them headed to the hospital.

When they arrived Bethany was still sobbing. The nurse signed her in and asked Ben and Annette to leave. They wouldn't be allowed to go any further with their daughter and would not be able to talk with her for three days. Only then could they come to visit for thirty minutes each day. Bethany screamed as Ben and Annette left and the nurses had to restrain her. She was officially admitted.

Ben felt badly as he left his only daughter in the care of the hospital staff but he knew it had to be done. Something was terribly wrong with her and he could no longer tolerate her actions. Annette felt relief as they left the building. Finally, something would be done to help their family. Both sat silently on the way home.

Bethany was so angry when her father left that she began yelling, screaming, and kicking anyone nearby. She was out of control so the nurses had to sedate her causing her to fall into a deep sleep until morning. The next day she awoke and began crying. She had been abandoned at a mental institution. She needed to call her mother . . . she would get her out of here. Bethany was not allowed to make any phone calls for the first twenty four hours. When she was finally able to make a call she immediately called Bell.

"Mamma, get me out of here!" she pleaded.

"Alright, baby, let me see what I can do." Bell replied.

Bell called the hospital administrator and begged them to let her pick up Bethany. They flatly refused stating that her father, who had custody rights, was the only one that was allowed to check her out. They explained that she would have to speak with the father.

This infuriated Bell. How dare Ben allow Annette to manipulate him into signing his only daughter into a nut house! Bell waited until the next phone call from Bethany. She explained to her daughter how to "play the game." Bell had been admitted into the psych ward many times and as long as the doctors thought the person was really trying hard they would release them sooner rather than later. Bethany agreed to try it.

Ben and Annette went to visit Bethany every day and each day she refused to see them. On the eighth day there Bethany finally agreed to a visit from them and seemed to be a totally different person. She was "playing the game" just as her mother had suggested. She was smiling and laughing the entire visit. The nurse stated that she had started to participate in group therapy and was progressing very well. Little did they know that Bethany hadn't changed at all . . . in fact, it had made her more determined than ever to do whatever she wanted to do. She just had to change the way she did things.

The phone rang early the next morning and Bell answered. It was Ms. Beasley. She told Bell that she was very sick and asked if she could come over for a little while. Bell had visited the woman on a weekly basis and she had been fine but Ms. Beasley had fallen and broken her leg so she was unable to get around very well. When Bell arrived she found the woman sitting in the chair with her leg in a cast propped up with the ottoman. Ms. Beasley was grateful to see Bell. She told her that she was having a hard time getting around and asked Bell for her help. Bell replied that she would be more than happy to help the woman with anything she needed. Ms. Beasley requested that Bell make them some tea.

"I have something I have wanted to talk to you about for some time now." She told Bell.

"Okay," said Bell, "Let me get us some hot tea and we'll have a chat."

Bell made the tea and opened the refrigerator to get some milk when she noticed that Ms. Beasley had insulin in the door. "I didn't know you're a diabetic," she said to the woman.

"Yes, unfortunately I haven't been able to get up to take it today. Do you mind, dear?"

"Not at all," replied Bell, "just tell me how to give it."

Ms. Beasley explained how to draw the drug up in a syringe and how to give the shot. Bell drew up the medicine and administered the insulin. She sat down in the chair by Ms. Beasley for their chat.

"I have been thinking about this a long time, Bell," she began. "As you know I have no family of my own and I consider you to be my family. That's why I met with my attorney last month to have everything put in your name. I'm getting older and want to be able to live my final days knowing that someone will appreciate what I have worked for all of my life. I hope you don't mind since I signed the power of attorney to you without discussing it with you first."

Bell was astonished. How easy was this? This old woman had fallen right into her plan. "I don't mind at all honey and I'm honored that you think of me as family," said Bell. Inside her head Bell was shouting for joy. The old bag had given Bell everything including her home, cars, and money. She knew that woman had a lot of money because she had seen some of the bank statements lying around. She thanked the woman; she didn't want to appear too eager so she had to contain her excitement. Bell picked up the dishes and headed to the kitchen to clean up. She even made Ms. Beasley a sandwich before she left after promising to return the next day.

Bell was on her way home when it hit her! Insulin! That's her key . . . she would have to look up the effects on the computer when she got home.

She found that everyone produces insulin although diabetics either don't produce enough or the insulin produced did not work properly. Here was the key. When she was ready she would give the old bag enough insulin to drop her blood sugar so low that she would go into a coma and die. Perfect! Now all Bell had to do is pick the time to put her plan into action. Wow! If she had only known about insulin before now! She loved the old woman's house and daydreamed about when she could move in. Maybe she would wait awhile . . .

Chapter 27

A couple of months later Bell decided it was time. Ms. Beasley was to have her cast removed at the end of the week so Bell needed to move forward before the woman was able to walk around again. She called Ms. Beasley to let her know she was on her way. Bell stopped by the bakery and bought a few pastries and headed to the old woman's house. When Bell arrived she gave Ms. Beasley a hug and went directly into the kitchen to make hot tea for their brunch. The woman was engrossed in her newspaper as Bell prepared the drinks. Bell opened the refrigerator and removed two vials of insulin. One vial was enough but Bell wanted to make sure the drug worked. She poured up two cups of tea, one with cream and sugar, the other with the two vials of insulin then placed the pastries on a plate and brought them to Ms. Beasley.

"Here you go, dear," she said politely.

Ms. Beasley smiled and thanked Bell for being so good to her. She sipped the tea slowly while she nibbled at the pastry. She finally finished her tea and asked for a refill in which Bell happily complied. A few minutes later Ms. Beasley became very pale in color and began to sweat even though her skin was cold as ice.

"Bell, I don't feel well," she stated. "Could you check my blood sugar?"

Bell pretended she hadn't heard the woman as she picked up the cups of tea and headed to the kitchen. She quickly washed the cups, dried them and put them away. When she returned to the living room Ms. Beasley had quietly slipped into a coma. Bell waited patiently until the old woman took her last breath. She gathered her things and headed home. The home health care nurse would arrive the next morning to find Ms. Beasley had died while reading her paper. It was so simple that Bell chuckled at her good luck. Of course Bell will act like she was devastated that the old girl died when in reality she was thrilled at her fortune.

Sure enough, the next morning the home healthcare nurse arrived at Ms. Beasley's home sharply at nine. She had her own key so she opened the door and called for the woman. When no one answered she made her way into the living room where she saw Ms. Beasley. The old woman was still sitting in her chair. The nurse immediately knew something was wrong; the woman was blue in color with mottled skin and had foamy drool down the side of her mouth. She felt for a pulse and found none. Ms. Beasley had obviously been dead for several hours. Her newspaper lay in her lap so the nurse assumed she had died while either reading the paper or during her sleep. The nurse called 911 and stated that she had found a diabetic patient dead upon her arrival. The ambulance came and took Ms. Beasley away. Knowing that the old woman had been close to Bell the nurse called her to give her the bad news.

Even though Bell sobbed and cried on the phone she was ecstatic inside. How easy it had been to get rid of the old woman and inherit money, cars, and another house! Now all she had to do is sit tight and play the part of losing a beloved friend. She didn't want to appear too anxious so she had to wait awhile to get the death certificate. As far as Bell knew Ms. Beasley didn't have any family so this should be easy.

Unfortunately for Bell Ms. Beasley did indeed have a daughter, Kim, who called the old woman everyday to check on her. Kim had been calling constantly with no answer when she became worried and called the Home Health Care service only to find that her mother had passed away. She had ensured several years ago that everything in her mother's name was changed to Kim's name so in essence, Ms. Beasley had nothing . . . not even a dime. Bell wasn't aware of this and began to clear some personal things out of the old woman's home when Ms. Beasley's daughter pulled into the driveway.

"Excuse me!" Stated Kim sharply, "What are you doing?"

"And who are you?" Bell replied angrily.

"Ms. Beasley was my mother and I don't appreciate someone pilfering through her things!"

"I'm very sorry for your loss but Ms. Beasley left everything to me in her will." Bell stated flatly as she continued to load the old woman's things in her car. Kim dialed 911 and requested the police department. She had blocked Bell from moving her car and in a matter of minutes the police arrived. They talked with both women and finally came to the conclusion that Bell was mistaken about the will and demanded she put everything back into the house. They told Bell that it was a matter for the courts. This made her furious; she was told by Ms. Beasley herself that everything the woman had was to be hers. She never mentioned having a daughter. Something was truly amiss. Bell skidded out of the driveway and headed for home. She needed Ms. Beasley's money and she intended to fight for what was hers!

Over the next few days Bell tried to get her hands on the paperwork that Ms. Beasley had mentioned but was unsuccessful. "Damn!" thought Bell, "I should have gotten that old woman's will before I gave her the insulin!"

Kim, on the other hand, had papers in hand when she had a locksmith change all the locks on her mother's home. She also filed a report with the police department in the event Bell tried to take anything from the house. Kim was an attorney and had an iron clad power of attorney dated less than a year ago. She decided to relocate her office and move into the home herself. Bell couldn't stand it. That house was hers along with the cars and money. She was the one who took care of the woman and she deserved everything! Bell had been deceived by this little old lady and she didn't like it at all but after her attorney reviewed both hers and Kim's legal documents he concluded that Bell's documents were invalid. Ms. Beasley had previously signed all of her rights over to her daughter and Bell would get nothing.

Bell was depressed. She had counted on getting an extremely large amount of money from Ms. Beasley. That old bitch cheated her! Kim thought she was so high class and better than Bell; she would somehow get even!

Ben and Annette were on their way to pick up Bethany. She was being released from the hospital after spending several weeks in therapy. Upon their arrival Bethany was sitting in her room waiting to go home. She smiled at Ben and ran to hug him. She totally ignored Annette and wouldn't even look at her. Her paperwork was complete and they could leave. Bethany walked beside her father telling him everything that had happened and how happy she was to get to go home. Annette followed behind allowing them to have their time together. When they got in the car Bethany leaned against the window and fell asleep. After an hour drive they arrived home. Much to Ben's surprise his daughter did not even acknowledge Annette's existence even though Annette tried to make small talk, the girl just ignored her completely.

"Annette's talking to you, Bethany," he stated.

"I know," she replied as she walked into the house. "My therapist said to block out any and all negativity and I'm doing exactly that."

Annette just looked at Ben and shook her head. It didn't matter, really; Annette knew that Bethany hated her and she had grown tired trying to get along with the girl."

Bethany immediately headed to her room to listen to music. She smiled to herself as she realized that this was actually going to be fun; making Annette uncomfortable in her own home was going to be so easy and as long as she wasn't disrespectful there was no way she could get into trouble with her dad. Everything was Annette's fault anyhow; her parents divorce, taking her away from her mother, all a result of Annette. Bethany had learned quite a bit in the psych unit but not from the counselors or doctors. She learned from the patients she shared her room with. They all had problems and taught Bethany how to deal with different situations. Her dad and Annette thought she was crazy? Well, she'll show them just what crazy is all about!

Annette and Ben sat down at the kitchen table both shocked at the way Bethany was acting. "Maybe the hospital stay has made her worse?" Ben stated.

"Worse? How much worse can you get when you torture a helpless little creature just for the fun of it?"

"Annette, I don't know what to do except let's wait and see how she acts for the next few days."

Bethany was extremely polite to Ben and just didn't say anything to Annette. If she were asked a question she would give a short, quick answer otherwise ignoring Annette completely.

Bell arrived to pick up Bethany for the weekend. She loved her daughter and was angry that the girl had to stay in the mental facility for so long. Bethany was happy to see her mother and ran outside to greet her. It had been a long time since the two of them saw each other.

Bell talked to Bethany late into the night listening to the happenings of each day she spent at the psychiatric hospital. Bethany told her mother what some of the patients were saying and Bell agreed with them. "You shouldn't have to speak to Annette if you don't want to," she told Bethany, "she's not your mother, just your daddy's whore."

Bethany knew her mother would understand. Actually, she was the only person that Bethany trusted completely even though she knew her mother was a pathological liar. That was something else that Bethany had inherited from her mother. Bethany hated Annette and she was thankful that she could talk with her mother about her feelings. Bethany loved her mother dearly and wished she could live with both her parents. If she could just get rid of Annette and Hunter maybe her father would let her mother move in the nice house with them. Bethany dreamed of that day.

Bell started feeling less depressed since she picked up her daughter. She had decided to surprise Bethany with a slumber party. Even though it was just the two of them she had ordered pizza and had a variety of snacks and drinks. They would talk for hours about everything that had happened in Bethany's life since she saw her last . . . just two crazy girls having a good time. Bethany told her mother that she considered her more of a "best friend" than a mother and was thrilled at the idea of a party. Mother and daughter ate, drank, and talked into the wee hours of the morning. Bethany told her mother everything that had happened in the psych unit. Bell was happy that her daughter wasn't speaking to Annette. Sooner or later Annette would get tired of it all and leave. This would allow Bell to get her husband back.

During the party Bethany opened her overnight bag and pulled out a brown paper bag with what appeared to be mail in it. To Bell's delight Bethany had stolen some of Annette's bills and financial statements. As she glanced through the envelopes she realized that her daughter had given her all of Annette's financial information including credit card numbers, bank account numbers and her social security number. What at find! Her daughter had completed a job well done!

After taking Bethany home the next day Bell had time to sit down and go through all the paperwork that her daughter had stolen. She found everything she needed to assume Annette's identity. Why shouldn't she? She was the rightful owner of the money that Ben had made and he was the one that paid the insurance, after all, he was her husband. Bell had needed to go to the doctor for a checkup so now she had an insurance card to pay for it. She would schedule it today! She also needed a new stove for her kitchen. She would order that today as well since she had Annette's credit card. It seemed like Christmas!

Bell's doctor visit went without any problems. They charged it to Ben's insurance without blinking an eye. She was so greedy that she didn't realize eventually Annette would find out about it. Bell went into a spending frenzy. She bought a new stove, a microwave oven, and things for Bethany. She was having so much fun that she inadvertently maxed out two of the four credit cards in the first day. She finished with the next two a couple of days later. Bell wasn't worried, if Annette called the police they wouldn't do anything to Bell since she had gotten away with so much already. It was amazing how easy it had been to charge everything on a credit card and she didn't even have to show her drivers license. "I just wish I could see the look on Annette's face when she finds out she has no credit left on any of her cards!" Bell thought as she laughed out loud, "and most of them were in Ben's name!"

Ben received a call from his Visa card company. "Hello sir, I am calling to inform you that your Visa card has been charged over the limit and we would like to know when to expect payment," the caller stated.

"What?" Ben exclaimed, "I have a ten thousand dollar limit on that card and I know I haven't used it at all this year!" Ben felt a familiar sick feeling in the bottom of his stomach.

"According to our records Annette used the card today which caused the card to be over limit."

"There must be some mistake, let me call my wife since she handles the bills," he replied and hung up. He immediately called Annette and repeated what the woman had told him. Annette told her husband that she had used the card to get gas but hadn't used it in months previously. Ben was very upset and couldn't believe his card was maxed out. Luckily, Annette had the day off and would find out what was going on.

When Annette found out that every one of their credit cards had been maxed out she had to sit down on the sofa. Her legs were weak and she was sick to her stomach. Tens of thousands of dollars were due on the four credit cards combined. What the hell was happening? She knew she hadn't charged much on them and she didn't believe Ben had either so who was using their credit cards? She immediately called the police who came to her house and took a report. They said the case would be turned over to an investigator within the next couple of days. Although Annette filed disputes with all the credit companies, it would take weeks if not months to fix the problem. By the time Ben arrived home he had become very angry. Who would do such a thing and how did they get the information? He and Annette both were extremely diligent in shredding all personal paperwork.

Annette went to her file folder and was astonished at what she didn't find. The folder was empty. She would keep each month's statements and bills in a small accordion file folder but found it completely empty. Someone had removed every shred of paper in the folder. Annette sat on the edge of the bed. There were only four people in the house. She didn't believe Hunter had anything to do with it, she was sure that neither she nor her husband had removed the files, so that left only one person . . . Bethany. Who else would have a reason to do this? How would she know what to take? Maybe that's why everything disappeared? Annette felt the heat inside her body rise as the anger grew greater and greater. This was it! She had been through enough and if she found out that the girl took the paperwork to Bell she would have them both prosecuted and she didn't care what Ben said about it! Annette stormed out of the bedroom and yelled for the children to come downstairs.

"Have either of you been in our bedroom?" she asked trying to calm down, "we are missing some very important papers."

"Not me!" exclaimed Hunter.

"Me neither," said Bethany.

"No one else has been in this house! Whoever took those papers has financially ruined me and your father! When I find out who did this, things will go very poorly for that person." As hard as Annette tried not to believe it was Bethany who took the papers she just couldn't make herself believe it was anyone else. She knew it had to be her. As the two children turned to go upstairs Bethany turned around and smiled at Annette as if to mock her.

Annette could feel her blood boil so much that she had to turn away before she did something she would regret. Now she was positive that Bethany had stolen the papers but she couldn't prove it. Annette's breathing became labored and she headed to her bedroom for an inhaler. After using her medicine she felt better but was still livid. How would Ben react? Would he believe that his only daughter actually smirked at the mention of financial devastation?

Ben came through the door in a rage. Annette relayed everything the credit card companies had told her then broke the news to him about the missing papers. Ben turned white in color and sat down. He felt like he was going to pass out. He sat silently for several minutes before picking up the phone and dialing the police department. Although Annette had filed appeals on all of the credit cards he wanted justice. Someone had used his cards and put his finances in jeopardy and he was sure that "someone" was Bell. He also realize that Bethany had to be the one who stole the papers but he was so angry that he couldn't deal with her right now. As soon as he hung up the phone with the police department he dialed his attorney's number. Ben was serious and out for blood!

Annette didn't mention the smirk that Bethany gave her when she heard that Annette had discovered the missing paperwork. She would let Ben have some time to cool down first. It was hard for Annette to control her anger toward the girl. In fact, she told Bethany that the best thing she could do would be to stay in her room for awhile. What in the world was wrong with that girl? Did she really have some type of autism or was she just plain mean? What could Ben and Annette do? Send her back to the crazy thief called her mother? For the second time today Annette began to have an asthma attack. She took her medicine and lay on the bed. Ben stretched out beside her and they both drifted off the sleep. Sleep . . . the only peaceful hours they would have for months to come.

They awoke with the sound of Hunter knocking on the door. "Something's wrong with Bethany!" he shouted in a panicked voice. Ben opened the door and found Hunter with a look of fear on his face.

Ben ran upstairs and found his daughter running around the room in circles, giggling. "Bethany!" shouted Ben, "What are you doing?"

"I'm running in the rain!" she said gleefully.

"No, you're not!" her father replied sternly.

"I'm an airplane!"

"Bethany, stop! You're acting crazy!" Bethany paid no attention to her father's demands. She kept running around in circles. Finally, Ben grabbed her and sat her on her bed. She couldn't even focus on what Ben was saying. She fell backwards on the bed laughing hysterically. Something was seriously wrong with the girl but what? Annette entered the room when Bethany squealed gleefully and repeated over and over, "Annette's here! Annette's here!" Annette didn't know what to do. In all her years of nursing she'd never seen anyone act like this. Maybe they should call an ambulance? Bethany suddenly became quiet while still smiling. She looked at Annette then back at her dad over and over again.

"Are you okay?" Ben asked.

"Sure, I'm just happy. I've realized that nobody can make me happy except myself and I've decided to be very, very happy."

Ben and Annette looked at each other. They were speechless. Ben told his daughter to calm down and both he and his wife left the room. "What the hell?" asked Ben, "What in the world is wrong with her?" Annette just shrugged her shoulders with a puzzled look on her face. She didn't know how to answer his question.

"We need to keep a close watch on her, Ben," she said, "something is terribly wrong and I don't know what's causing it." Ben nodded his head in agreement. Both he and Annette were at their wits end and didn't know where to go to get help.

Annette called the psychiatric hospital the next day and spoke with the doctor. According to him they should be happy that Bethany was not depressed or suicidal and that it was normal for children to act silly at times. Annette wasn't buying any of it. She knew something was deeply wrong with her step daughter and she wasn't sure what was causing it. Maybe she would speak with some of the doctors at the hospital where she worked although she didn't like taking her personal problems to the workplace.

Bethany seemed more normal and never mentioned last night's outburst. She was friendly and polite to Annette and even invited Hunter to play board games with her. "It's like she's a different child," thought Annette as she watched the two children play. Annette had other things to worry about at the moment. She had cancelled all of her credit cards and she and Ben were meeting with their attorney to get their financial house back in order. Annette was sure that this time the police would arrest Bell. She had to be the one behind the scheme to steal their information and ruin their credit. No one else could have gotten that information. They were too overwhelmed to deal with Bethany whom Annette was sure stole the papers.

Bell sat on the sofa and laughed out loud at the thought of Ben and Annette struggling to fix their finances. There was no way they could trace the purchases back to her. She had any deliveries sent to the abandoned house near her job and she only used the computers at the library to order the merchandise. They may suspect that Bell had committed the crime but they couldn't prove anything. It made her feel like she had finally given Annette and Ben a little pay back for all the things they had done to her.

Once the police completed their investigation it turned out exactly like Bell had predicted. They suspected that she was the culprit but couldn't prove it. The case was closed. Ben and Annette were furious. Once again, Bell had slipped through the cracks and gotten away with a crime. It would take months for the attorney to get the couple's finances returned to normal. They were informed that thousands of people per year had to deal with stolen identities and financial theft and although it was a great imposition at least they still had some money left in their bank account. It was no comfort for Ben and Annette.

Bethany was going to visit her mother for a week against Ben's wishes, however, Annette had voiced to her husband that even though it probably wasn't a good idea for the girl to spend a prolonged period of time with her mother at least Annette could have a week of sanity. He finally agreed. At the time Annette was all for Bethany going to Bell's house but she would later live to regret it. Bethany was excited to leave and didn't even bother saying goodbye as she ran out the door. Annette gave a sigh of relief as she watched Bell pull out of the driveway.

A week passed quickly and Bethany finally arrived home and was in quite a mood. She headed straight upstairs to her room without saying a word. She came down to eat dinner but still wasn't speaking to anyone; just glaring at anybody who passed her way. Annette could tell that the girl was upset but she just didn't have the energy to ask her what was wrong. Bethany finished her dinner and again, without a word, headed to her room.

The next day Bethany came downstairs and although she still appeared to be sullen, asked Annette to take her shopping. "I will take you Bethany, but not today."

Bethany slammed her hand against the counter and shouted, "I need new clothes . . . today!"

"That's enough!" said Annette firmly

"My mom said it was your job to buy me clothes and I need them today!" the girl screamed.

"No! Now go to your room"

Bethany burst into tears and ran upstairs where she stayed until Ben came home. She quietly came downstairs and smiled at her father. "Daddy, I want to go shopping. Will you take me tomorrow?"

"We'll see sweetie," he replied, "we will make sure you have what you need but I can't promise you it will be tomorrow. We'll see."

Annette was fit to be tied. She had already told her husband how Bethany had acted and now he's implying that she's going to get to go shopping soon. Annette had already told her no! She cut her eyes hard at Ben and scowled. He apparently didn't see his wife's reaction as he continued.

"I know that new clothes are important to you and I want you to have them but sometimes you may have to wait a day or two until we're off from work."

"I understand, Daddy," Bethany replied sweetly. She turned toward Annette so her father couldn't see and smiled a big toothy smirk as if to say, "See there? I can get my way anytime I want to!"

Annette was too tired to argue with Ben. She had talked to him until she was blue in the face and although she knew he just wanted to keep the peace but she felt betrayed. Annette had grown tired and weary of Bethany's behavior. She had done everything in her power to help the girl but to no avail. Bethany wanted things her way and was not going to budge even little bit. Bethany nagged Annette from the time that she arrived home until time to go to bed about things she wanted and needed as well as asking Annette to take her places. It was apparent that Bethany had been told by her mother to annoy Annette as much as possible in the hopes that Annette would grow tired of it and leave. Annette wasn't leaving.

She spoke with her husband about how she felt and they both agreed that they could not go on living in such turmoil. They both knew that Bethany was behind most of the problems and drama that they had to deal with on a daily basis. After several days of thought on the matter Ben and Annette decided that the best place for Bethany was with her mother. They would send her to Bell's house before school started again for the year. It was not a decision that came easily. They desperately wanted to help Bethany but she firmly believed the stories that her mother told and didn't want to hear anything different.

Ben and Annette sat with Bethany and told her what they had decided. The girl didn't flinch, instead she told them that she hated them both and she would pray that something bad would happen to them. She admitted how much she hated Hunter and was happy when Annette lost the baby and her only regret was that Annette hadn't broken her neck when she fell. Bethany was on a roll! She said that Bell was the only person in the world she cared about and she hadn't wanted to move in with Ben and Annette from the start. By this time Bethany was screaming, "I hope you both die!" Ben couldn't hear anymore. He grabbed his daughter and shook her hard telling her to be quite. He marched her to his car and shoved her in the passenger seat then drove her to Bell's house where he pulled her out of the car and left her on her mother's front lawn.

Ben was shaking so hard he couldn't keep hold of the steering wheel. He felt his flushed face as he tried to calm down. How could his own flesh and blood look him in the eye and tell him she wished he were dead? Where had he gone wrong as a parent? Ben couldn't go home just yet. He had to get control of his anger first. He had never dreamed that his daughter would speak to him like that! He then thought of his wife. She hadn't laughed in months and he missed that laughter. Had the recent stress changed her? Annette used to be such a caring person but lately he hadn't seen that side of her either. He saw a haggard, overworked woman who seemed to be going through the day to day chores like a robot. Suddenly guilt took the place of anger. He had just left his only daughter at Bell's house to suffer the wrath of her mother. How could he have done this? It was obvious that Bethany had severe mental issues like Bell but she was still his child.

Ben turned into his driveway and parked the car. He sat silently for a few minutes until he could muster up enough strength to go inside. He felt mentally and physically drained. His emotions were out of control as he fell onto the sofa and sobbed. Annette heard him and put her arms around her husband to comfort him. They both sat for hours without saying a word. Annette couldn't cry for Bethany; in fact she was glad the girl was gone. Bethany had been so hateful when her father wasn't around and Annette knew that she was the cause of her losing her baby. As far as Bethany was concerned Annette believed the girl deserved to spend the rest of her childhood with the crazy woman who is her mother. They deserved each other. Annette then thought about the life that the girl would have and felt guilty by even thinking such things. All the daily turmoil had changed Annette; she never dreamed she would feel this way about any child much less her own step daughter. What had happened to her? Why couldn't she control her feelings? Was there darkness inside everyone that just didn't manifest itself until awakened?

The next morning began with bright sunshine warming the bedroom as Annette and Ben awoke. The house was so quiet that they had slept late but it was Saturday and who cared? They had a peaceful day planned and would just stay home this weekend and do chores around the house and get plenty of well needed rest. Ben had conflicting feelings about his daughter being gone. On one hand, his family's life would be calmer but on the other hand he had sent his daughter to live with a lunatic.

Bell was up early as she decided to surprise her daughter with her favorite breakfast, pancakes. Bethany was already up and dressed and she too had a surprise for her mother. She had cooked bacon and eggs for Bell. They sat down and enjoyed their breakfast. They discussed the actions of Ben and Annette while they made fun of Hunter. Bell and Bethany both hated Annette and Hunter and would make snide remarks about them both then laugh at themselves. It was no secret to Bethany that her mother was still in love with her father. Bell made it clear that Ben belonged with her.

Both Bethany and Bell were living in a fantasy world. Just because Bethany had come to live with her mother didn't mean that she had given up hope that Annette would leave. She would go visit them every other weekend and make their lives a complete hell on earth. That was her plan. They had kicked her out of their home and they would pay dearly for it! Bethany was restless so she decided to go for a run. She took off down the street and around the corner. She suddenly stopped in her tracks. On the sidewalk was the cutest little kitten she had ever seen. She picked it up and ran towards home with the kitten in her arms. She came racing into the house to show her mother.

"Mom! Look what I found!" she yelled loudly.

"I see," said Bell, "and what do you intend to do with it?

"I want to keep it, of course!" she replied.

"Okay, Bethany, but you're going to have to be the one to take care of it."

"Oh yes, I definitely will!" Bethany squealed with happiness.

As Bell watched the kitten she felt the darkness rising up within her. She hadn't been around an animal for a long time. She couldn't wait for school to start so she could be home alone with the kitten. Oh what fun she would have!

Chapter 28

The day finally came about two weeks later. She had just seen Bethany onto the school bus knowing it would be the afternoon before her daughter returned home. Bethany had been taking care of the kitten; she even named it Pixie. Bell sat down on the sofa as Pixie jumped up on her lap to be caressed. Bell had decided that since the cat was going to live inside it needed declawing. Bell wasn't about to spend money on a veterinarian so she would declaw the kitten herself. How hard could it be? She wrapped the kitten tight in gauze so it couldn't move. She then took a pair of pliers and began removing the claws. The poor cat screamed as Bell yanked out claw after claw. Blood was everywhere. Bell's heart rate increased and she began to breath faster. She enjoyed this! Bell snatched out the last claw but wasn't done with the torture. She took the kitten to the kitchen where she kept her biggest, sharpest knife. She promptly cut off the animal's tail. "Ah! Now we have a bob cat!" Bell exclaimed. The kitten was so weak it could barely move until Bell poured rubbing alcohol onto the wounds. The animal was still screaming as it ran into the bedroom to hide. The tiny animal's heart was pounding as it shook in fear under Bethany's bed.

When Bethany arrived home Bell told her that she had taken the cat to the vet to get declawed and have its tail removed. Bethany believed her mother as she rushed into the bedroom to check on her cat. Bethany found her beloved pet under her bed curled up into what looked like a little furry ball. She gently picked up the kitten and laid it on her bed.

The kitten had been exhausted and finally fell asleep. The bleeding had stopped and dried blood covered each little paw as well as its tail. Bethany left it alone to recover.

Bell decided to contact her attorney. If Bethany was going to live with her she needed a hefty child support check every month from Ben. She knew Ben and Annette both had good jobs and made a substantial amount of money so they could easily afford giving some of that money to her. She would need it to raise her daughter. Bell's attorney said he would begin the paperwork immediately. Bell also demanded that in addition to the monthly child support, Ben would pay for all extracurricular activities, maintain insurance, and buy all clothing for his daughter. He would also pay for Bethany's college expenses for four years. Bell smiled as she was quite pleased with the thought of extra money coming in.

It took the poor kitten a couple of weeks to recover from its traumatic experience. Its tail had finally started healing as well as its paws. Although Pixie loved attention the animal was very skittish around Bell. When Bethany would leave to go to school the kitten couldn't be found. It would hide under Bethany's dirty clothes until she arrived back home. Even though Pixie was a small animal it still understood the pain associated with Bell and tried to avoid her at all costs. If Bell walked into the room While Bethany was playing with her kitten the animal would hiss and run under the furniture. This would strike the normal person as being odd but Bethany never noticed the animal's strange behavior.

Bethany loved being at her mother's house. She could do whatever she wanted and Bell didn't care. It was actually the first time in years that Bell bought her daughter new clothes. Bell was happy to have her at home; they were more like best friends rather than mother and daughter. Bethany and Bell would spend each evening talking about their feelings. Bell confided in her daughter that she would always love Ben and would still do anything to have him back. Bethany would console her mother and reassure her that Ben left because of Annette and had nothing to do with Bell.

Bell had spent months trying to find a way to make some extra money. She finally decided that if she took in an elderly bedridden patient she would not only get paid for the patient's care but could manipulate any money they had. A perfect idea! Bell put the word out at the nursing home where she worked as well as to all her friends at the church. One day she received a call from a family that needed someone to care for their mother whom had suffered a stroke and couldn't speak. Bell jumped on it; she felt that this would be the ideal person to share her home with. The family moved their mother in Bell's home the following weekend.

Not only could Ms. Davis not speak but she was completely at the mercy of her caregiver. She was bedridden; she couldn't walk or even roll over in the bed without assistance. She could, however, feed herself if provided with food. Bell was thrilled! She had cleaned her house and spruced up the spare bedroom for her guest. The family was from out of town and didn't know Bell but they had heard about her from their relatives whom attended the same church as Bell.

The first night wasn't bad as the exhausted woman slept most of the time. The next day Bell walked into the room to check on Ms. Davis and the smell of feces hit her in the face. The old woman had defecated and the feces had leaked onto the bed. Bell called for Bethany to help as they cleaned the woman and help her put on clean pajamas. Bethany left to go to school so Bell decided to make things clear to her guest.

"You are NOT allowed to shit on my bed!" screamed Bell. "You are an adult and need to act like it!"

Bell placed a garbage bag around the woman's lower torso in the event of another accident. Ms. Davis was so ashamed she couldn't even look at Bell. For lunch Bell made soup in a cup and a straw for the patient to sip from. She gave her orange juice to drink. The soup wasn't even warm but the old woman was so hungry she drank all the cold soup then fell asleep. She was frightened of Bell and didn't want to do anything to make her mad.

As days turned into weeks Bell created a routine for her guest. She would set soup on a tray next to the bed and return an hour later when Ms. Davis was asleep. Bell was enjoying playing nurse although she wasn't very good at it. She hated changing the old woman's diaper but at least she didn't have to change the sheets anymore. The garbage bag worked great. She really didn't even have to cook either; just open a can of soup and sit it on the tray. Maybe she would give Ms. Davis a special treat of ice cream. All old people like ice cream.

Ms. Davis' family only came to see her about once a month. During those times Bell would remove the garbage bag and make sure her patient was clean and well fed. Bell would dote on Ms. Davis while the family was there only to return to her ways when they left. One day, when Bell was in one of her moods, Ms. Davis accidentally wet her entire bed. Bell was so angry that she slapped the old woman hard across the face. Ms. Davis cried herself to sleep that night.

After several months passed the family's visits became fewer and farther between. Bell was getting tired of taking care of Ms. Davis even though she received a large check each week for the woman's care. The old woman smelled of urine and feces because Bell refused to change her every time she used her adult diaper. Ms. Davis was continuing to get soup twice a day and nothing else. Every once in a while Bethany would go into Ms. Davis' room and fill her mouth with hot peppers. Bethany would laugh when the woman struggled with the burning sensation from the peppers. Bell would laugh too and tell Bethany to "do it again!" They would make the poor soul swallow the peppers before they would give her a drink of water. Sometimes they wouldn't allow her any water at all.

Bell enjoyed this more than usual. She could feel the darkness well up inside her when she realized that torturing a human would be the ultimate rush. Bell had always tortured animals but this would far outreach the feeling she would get from a puppy or kitten. She would have to plan something spectacular!

Bethany brought home her boyfriend to meet Bell. Bethany was now fifteen years old and her boyfriend, Nick, was twenty. Bell was a little wary about this new friend but relaxed after meeting him. He was very polite and soft spoken, tall and lanky. He had met Bethany through his younger sister and although he knew he was too old for Bethany he couldn't help but like her . . . a lot. Bell was okay with the age difference, in fact she herself was slightly attracted to this young man but she would never let her daughter know it. Nick began dating Bethany on a regular basis and often spent days at her house. He would stay at Bell's while Bethany attended school. Bell liked the company and would actually put her "sexy" dress on when she knew he would be spending the day. Nick liked the idea that two different women were doting on him.

One day while Bethany was at school Bell was in an unusually happy mood. She dressed in her finest dress and walked in the living room. She began swaying from side to side towards Nick as she unbuttoned the front of the dress. Nick appeared to enjoy the show and met Bell in the middle of the room. They embraced as he steered her toward the bedroom. They spent the entire day in bed until it was time for Bethany to come home from school. Nick showered and dressed to await his next conquest. Bell felt a little guilty since Nick was Bethany's boyfriend but Bethany was a girl and Nick needed a real woman and he certainly didn't seem to mind.

After several months Nick was practically living with Bell and Bethany. It became a routine that when Bethany left to go to school Nick would come into Bell's bedroom to spend the morning. Ms. Davis was pretty much left alone until the afternoon. She no longer received any type of breakfast and received cold soup for lunch. If she was lucky Bell would make something quick for dinner. The old woman's health was declining rapidly. She had lost ten pounds and didn't have much strength. Although Ms. Davis had lost her ability to speak and move herself around she still have the ability to think for herself. She knew that unless something drastic happened she was going to die in Bell's house.

Chapter 29

B en hadn't seen his daughter in months even though he and Annette had invited her to visit frequently. The only time he even spoke to his daughter is when she called to ask for money. His guilt from sending her to her mother's house had been eating at him for a long time. He felt he had sealed his own daughter's fate forever. He was fully aware of his wife's opinions regarding Bethany but he didn't necessarily agree with her although he understood why she felt the way she did. Ben missed his time with Bethany. There was a time when she thought her father was the greatest man in the world; not anymore. In fact, Bethany had come to the opinion that her father was mean and unreasonable. Ben had to learn that Bethany will make her own fate and it had nothing to do with him.

Annette and Ben's relationship had improved a great deal since Bethany moved in with her mother even though they didn't discuss the girl very often. Ben believed that he had made a terrible mistake when he forced his daughter to leave. Annette, on the other hand, was convinced that being at her mother's house was exactly what Bethany needed. Although Hunter missed having another kid around he was glad his sister moved.

Bell walked in to Ms. Davis' room where the drapes were always drawn so the darkness enveloped the room twenty four hours a day. She opened the drapes wide as the bright sunshine shone through the windows. Ms. Davis squinted as the bright light hit her in the face. Bell was up to something, she was sure of it. Bell was unusually happy today as she was softly humming a song as she made herself busy tidying up the room. The old woman still wore a garbage bag around her pelvis in the event she became incontinent. Bell and Bethany had to stop stuffing hot peppers in Ms. Davis' mouth as they began to upset the woman's stomach. It was funny, however, to watch her struggle with the burning sensation of the peppers when they burned her mouth and throat. Ms. Davis' face would get really red and she would start sweating. Since Bell was in such a good mood today she would paint Ms. Davis' fingernails for her. Bell gathered the nail polish and began to apply a thick, sticky coat to the old woman's nails. As she stroked bright red polish on each nail Bell had an idea. After she completed all ten fingers and toes Bell picked up a small piece of wood she had collected from outside. She tore off a small splinter and shoved in under Ms. Davis' thumbnail. The woman moaned in pain as Bell continued the torture until every fingernail throbbed. Tears flowed down the poor woman's cheek as she heard Bell say, "This is to make sure you know you're alive, Old Woman!" Bell was still laughing when she pulled the drapes closed and turned off the lights. The darkness was taking over and she reveled in it.

That night Ms. Davis couldn't sleep. Every time she made the slightest movement her fingers would throb in pain. "How could anyone be so cruel?" she thought. "How much am I going to have to suffer before I die?" Ms. Davis wished she were dead so she could get some kind of relief from the agony. Her fingers had swollen as the splinters caused inflammation under the nails. This was literally hell on earth. If only she could talk and be able to tell someone what was happening! How could anyone do these horrible things? Finally, the pain was so overwhelming that Ms. Davis slipped into unconsciousness.

A couple of days later Ms. Davis awoke to the throbbing in her fingers. Fortunately, the splinters had caused such infection that they slipped out from under her nails. The poor old woman couldn't see very well because Bell had taken her glasses away but she could tell that they were gone. Maybe she was over the worst of the torture . . . but she doubted it.

Bethany came in the old woman's room to bring her soup. She also removed the trash bag around Ms. Davis' pelvis so her mother could change the bedding. Bethany laid her phone on the nightstand by the bed as she removed the bag and placed it in the trash can. She then left the room and shouted loudly to her boyfriend who was leaving, "Wait! I want to go too!" Ms. Davis heard the door slam as she turned her head toward the cell phone. Now was her chance! She picked up the phone and immediately dialed 911.

"911 operator four what is your emergency?" Ms. Davis couldn't speak.

"This is 911 do you have an emergency?" There was silence on the end of the line. Ms. Davis tapped on the phone.

"I'm tracing you're location and will send the police." The operator stated, "Please stay on the phone."

Ms. Davis was trembling. Finally, someone would come to save her!

Belle heard the sirens and as she looked out the window she saw emergency vehicles pulling into her driveway. The loud knock on the door startled Bell. She opened the door to see two policemen on her porch.

"Hello, ma'am" one stated. We received an open line call from this address. "Is everything alright?"

"Why of course!" Bell exclaimed. I didn't call anyone.

"May we come in and look around?"

Bell was nervous and hoped the officers didn't notice but she had to let them in.

"Who all is in the home?" the officer asked.

"Just myself and the elderly lady I'm taking care of" Bell replied.

"May we speak with her?" they asked.

"You may see her but she can't talk. She had a stroke some time ago and it affected her speech. She's also very demented." stated Bell as she escorted them to Ms. Davis' room. Bell held her breath as they walked into the room. Thankfully, Bethany had removed the trash bag from the old woman.

"Hello," stated the officer, "is everything okay?"

Ms. Davis was so excited to see that help had arrived she began to sob. She kept pointing at her fingers trying to show them they had been injured but the policeman didn't understand.

"She really doesn't know what she's doing," Bell said flatly. Then she saw her daughter's cell phone.

"Ms. Davis," Bell said sweetly, "honey, you shouldn't have called 911 if you didn't have an emergency. You've brought these nice men here for nothing and they're very busy." She turned to the police officers and said, "I'm so sorry she called you guys. She gets excited every once in a while."

"No problem, we're glad everyone is okay. Thank you for letting us in your home. We'll be on our way."

Bell showed them to the door and watched them leave. She was livid! How dare that old bat call the cops on her! Bell stormed into Ms. Davis' bedroom. "You called the cops on me after all I've done for you? You old hag, you will pay dearly for this!" Bell slammed the bedroom door as she left.

Bell was still upset when Nick arrived. He took her in his arms to console her and guided her to the bedroom. After an hour or so of intimate passion Nick stretched his arms and bragged, "I am certainly king of this household; I've serviced every woman in this house."

"Not EVERY woman," Bell stated as she smiled. Bell pointed to Ms. Davis' bedroom, "so . . . really, you are NOT king of this household.

Nick immediately knew what she meant. "We'll see about that," he stated as he headed toward the old woman's room. "I'll show her what a real man is!" He left Ms. Davis' door open so Bell could watch.

Soon Bell heard muffled screams coming from the old woman's room. Nick was doing exactly what Bell wanted. "That will teach the bitch to call the cops," she thought. Bell began to smile with sweet revenge. The darkness inside had engulfed her and was trying to take over her every move. Nick came out after a few minutes and declared that now he indeed had conquered every woman in the home.

Chapter 30

Ben and Annette had been so stressed for such a long period of time that they decided they needed a break. They would take a few days off from work and go to the mountains. It was turning into the fall season and Ben knew that this was Annette's favorite time of the year. They would take Hunter as well since he too had suffered. Ben had rented a log cabin deep in the mountains so they could swim in the lake, go boating, and just relax. As he helped his wife pack for the trip he noticed how tired she looked. She had lost that happy twinkle in her eyes and hardly ever smiled anymore. Maybe this trip would change that. Ben felt lucky to have her to stand by him through thick and thin. Would she have still married him knowing what hell they would have to go through? Ben wasn't sure but was deeply grateful that she was here by his side.

Annette packed their belongings like a robot. She felt numb and stressed out. She hoped the trip would rejuvenate their family. It had been a long time since they went anywhere and she thought Ben was very thoughtful and sweet to make all the arrangements. Annette loved her husband and knew that they could be happy together for the rest of their lives but something kept nagging at her. She wasn't sure exactly what it was but she had the feeling of impending doom. Maybe she was just being silly since she had worked a very stressful shift the night before. Anyways, the mountains sounded great and she could hardly wait to get there. Hunter ran downstairs with his suitcase in hand. He was so excited he couldn't be still so Annette sent him outside to play for awhile while she and Ben completed their packing. Ben was placing the last suitcase in the care when his phone rang. The hospital in a nearby county was calling to inform Ben that his daughter had overdosed. He was needed at the emergency room as soon as possible. Ben's heart sank. He would have to go to Bethany. Ben explained the situation to Annette and Hunter. He saw the disappointment in their eyes but Annette told him it was okay. They could go to the mountains another time. She said she and Hunter would accompany him to the hospital.

When Ben walked into the emergency room he saw his daughter restrained to the bed yelling obscenities at everyone who walked in. When she saw her father she began to cry. Ben held her hand and comforted her. Annette stood by and watched as Bethany sobbed in her father's arms.

"Bethany, honey, what happened?" he asked.

"Daddy, please can I talk to you alone?" She glanced at Annette.

Annette took the hint and replied, "I'll wait in the waiting room." She promptly left Ben to speak with his daughter.

Bethany began to tell what happened. She had become ill at school so a friend brought her home early. When she walked into the house she didn't see anyone but she heard voices from her mother's bedroom. She walked to the bedroom and saw the door ajar. She peeked in the room and saw her boyfriend and her mother in the heat of passion. She was so overwrought that she didn't say anything to them. She just ran away and called her friend. When she arrived at the friend's house she was so upset she went directly to the bathroom where she found several types of prescription medicine in the cabinet. She took them all. Her friend found her passed out in the bathroom and called an ambulance. The next thing she remembered is when the emergency room staff put the tube up her nose and into her stomach to pump the medicine out.

Ben just sat there with his mouth open. He couldn't believe it! What kind of mother would do that to their child? Who was this piece of trash called Nick?

"Daddy, I don't have anywhere to go. What am I going to do?"

"You'll come home with me and Annette," replied Ben. Just then the doctor came in and sat down. He introduced himself and explained that Bethany would have to spend seventy two hours at the mental hospital for evaluation. Bethany would spend the night in the emergency room and be transferred first thing in the morning. He paused and then said, "Bethany, our tests results show something else that I don't know that you're aware of," he said, "you're pregnant."

Ben almost fell out of his chair. He couldn't believe what he'd just heard. His daughter had been through enough already and now she was pregnant! Bethany looked like she'd seen a ghost. The doctor abruptly left the room to see another patient and Bethany broke into tears again. "Daddy, what am I supposed to do?" she pleaded.

"I'll stay with you tonight and when you get out of the mental hospital you will come back home and live with me and Annette."

This seemed to satisfy the girl and she drifted off to sleep. Ben slipped out of her room and met Annette in the lobby. He explained what had happened and that he would spend the night. "She has no place to go when she gets out, Annette, so I asked her to come home with us." Annette wasn't sure she had heard correctly.

"Come home with us to live?" she asked

"Of course, she's pregnant with my grandchild. I can't just let her live in the streets," Ben sternly replied.

"Ben, have you forgotten what we've been through with that girl?"

"That girl, as you say, is my daughter!"

"Just please give me the keys, Ben, I'm tired." He handed his wife the keys and said he'd catch a cab in the morning.

"I won't be there, Ben," she replied, "I'm taking Hunter and we're going to drive to the cabin. I have to get away."

"Just wait until in the morning and I will drive you there."

"Whatever," she said as she headed out the exit. In her mind she was determined that she would go tonight. She didn't care if Ben liked it or not. This was supposed to be a special trip for the family. Annette had carefully planned for it only to be once again disappointed. She needed Ben's full attention since she was going to give him some wonderful news . . . she was pregnant! Not so wonderful now that she found out Bethany was pregnant as well. Annette had a lot to think about while Hunter slept as she drove the sixty miles to the mountain cabin. During the drive she let her mind wander. How could she allow Bethany to come into their home after she murdered their unborn baby? What was Ben thinking? She would protect this child she was carrying no matter what her husband said but she didn't want to argue with him in the hospital. Since Bethany was going to be confined to the mental hospital at least this would give

Annette a few of days to change his mind; that is, if he bothers to call. Regardless, Annette needed this trip more than ever.

Ben arrived home the next day only to find that Annette and Hunter never came home. He tried to call his wife but kept getting her voicemail. He started to panic; what if his family had left him for good? He couldn't even imagine life without Annette and Hunter so he called every hour for most of the day when he decided he would go find his wife. Ben drove his truck to the cabin in hopes of finding them there.

Bell wasn't aware of what happened to Bethany until Ben called her the next day. He was screaming at her as he told Bethany's story. He was so angry that after telling Bell where Bethany was transferred, he abruptly hung up the phone. He had fulfilled his duty and didn't want to hear Bell's whiny voice. Ben was driving faster than normal but he was anxious to get to his family by sun down.

Bell brought Ms. Davis' daily soup and set it on her bedside table. She opened the drapes when she noticed that the old woman didn't look very well. She felt her cold hands then realized that she was dead. Ms. Davis' heart gave out during the brutal attack. Bell didn't know it until the next afternoon. "Damn!" Bell really didn't want to lose the steady money coming every week but at least now she wouldn't have to wipe the old woman's ass. She had ensured that Ms. Davis prearranged everything should would need for her funeral so she called the funeral home to have them pick up the body. She didn't worry about any questions since the woman had been ill for such a long time. No one would ever know what happened.

Ben arrived at the cabin just as it was starting to get dark outside. He saw Annette's car in the driveway and breathed a sigh of relief. He jumped out of the car and ran to the door just as his wife opened it.

"I'm sorry honey," he said, "I've been insensitive and stupid. Please don't be mad. I love you"

Annette couldn't stay mad at Ben for long; she loved him dearly. She hugged him tightly and whispered, "I love you too." They both knew they had a lot to talk about but not tonight. Tonight they just wanted to hold each other; everything else could wait until tomorrow.

Bethany had been in the mental hospital for two days now. She wasn't happy at all and after being told she wouldn't be able to leave for another week or so. Nick had been to visit. He told Bethany that her mother had forced herself on him and informed him that she would not allow Bethany to date him unless he followed her wishes. He said that Bell blackmailed him. She would call the police since Bethany was underage. Well, today Bethany would turn seventeen; an adult in her state. She told Nick that she was pregnant. Nick asked her to elope and marry him. He had been so convincing that Bethany agreed. She knew her mother and it didn't surprise her that Bell would take advantage of the situation. She would move in with Nick upon her release from the hospital and they would get married. She never wanted to see her mother again and she wouldn't be forced to move in with her father and the bitch he married.

Bell came to see Bethany several times but her daughter refused to see her. Bell had come up with a very convincing story if Bethany would only listen. Bell didn't believe she had done anything wrong. It was all Nick's fault. He was the one who instigated the affair and he went along with it for months. Wait until Bethany finds out that Bell wasn't the only one in the home that Nick had been with! Bell was angry that this man came into their life and turned her only daughter against her. One way or the other she would make him pay!

Annette and Ben awoke late the next day since both of them were exhausted. They ate breakfast then took Hunter to the lake to swim. As they watched him Ben began to talk.

"Annette, I just don't know what to do. Bethany is pregnant at seventeen years old and she doesn't have anywhere to live. I told her she could live with us but I know how you feel about her. If I'm going to lose you because of her then I will try to find an alternative."

Annette didn't say anything for a few minutes. She appeared deep in thought. Finally, she said, "Ben, you know I love you . . . but I refuse to live with her and if she moves in Hunter and I will leave." There, she had said it. Now she waited for her husband's reaction. Maybe she should tell him right away that they were expecting a baby of their own but the timing just didn't seem right. She would wait.

Ben was shocked. How could his beautiful, loving wife feel this way about his daughter? After all, Bethany was a part of him and Annette seemed to hate her. "Honey, I know that the two of you have some issues but she's homeless! I don't want you to leave; I love you! Am I supposed to let her live in the streets?"

"She can continue to live with her mother, Ben. Do you not remember the turmoil within our home when she lived there? I just can't deal with that anymore." Annette started to become angry and hurt. She felt betrayed by her own husband. How could he not see that this girl was evil? Was he that blind to the situation? She was glad she hadn't mentioned her pregnancy.

Ben was annoyed. What did his wife expect him to do? Send Bethany back to Bell after she had slept with Bethany's boyfriend? He just couldn't do that. "Look, we'll come up with something. Let's not ruin our vacation."

"You already have, Ben." Annette got up and headed to the cabin. She felt nauseated and was about to vomit. She had to lie down for a few minutes until the feeling went away. This pregnancy was going to be tough with all the stress. She had to protect her unborn child no matter what.

Ben let Hunter swim for awhile longer then called for him to come in. It was getting late and almost time for dinner. Ben had calmed down and was racking his brain on what to do. He was torn between his wife whom he loved dearly and his daughter, his own flesh and blood. He had never seen Annette seem so cold hearted toward anyone. Maybe he can talk some sense into her.

When Ben and Hunter arrived at the cabin Annette had dinner waiting. She was still nauseated from the aroma of food but she didn't dare let on. They sat down to eat. Ben would keep the conversation light so he didn't irritate his wife. Hunter wasn't saying much; he was worn out from the day of swimming. Annette was unusually quite so Ben just rambled on and on trying to keep the conversation going. He wouldn't say anymore about Bethany until tomorrow.

Annette was in a good mood the next day so Ben decided to wait until later to broach the touchy subject again. The three of them went hiking on the mountain and had a picnic by the waterfall. The sky was a brilliant blue; the trees were glistening in the sun with colors of bright yellow, orange and red. Although the nights were cool the days were warm and comforting. Ben noticed how relaxed his wife appeared. This was the Annette he knew and loved; he felt closer to his wife at this moment that he had in the past couple of months.

The next day was the last day of vacation and the couple hadn't discussed their situation since the second day of vacation. They both knew they would have to talk about it but neither one could bring themselves to mention it. They would wait until they returned home.

Bell had repeatedly called Ben but didn't get an answer. She had fallen into a deep depression; the man she loved had remarried, her daughter wouldn't even speak to her and the young man that she shared her bed with was gone. She was all alone.

Ben and Annette finally returned home. The unloaded their vehicles and made a quick sandwich. Ben finally brought up the subject. "Annette, please understand where I'm coming from. I can't just throw my only child in the streets."

"Ben," Annette began trying to control her temper, "I've already told you that if Bethany moves in Hunter and I will leave. She's already poisoned Hunter and caused my miscarriage. I can't believe that you're so blind you don't see it!"

"You're not being fair! You're asking me something that I can't do! Bethany is supposed to get out of the hospital tomorrow and I plan to pick her up. I'm sorry, Annette, but I'm her father and it's my responsibility." Ben got up and headed to the shower. He didn't want to fight anymore. Annette went to bed. If that was his final word then she would do whatever was necessary to protect her children.

The next morning Ben left early to pick up Bethany. Annette jumped out of bed as soon as she heard him leave. It would take her husband and hour or so with traffic to get to the hospital. By the time he returned her and Hunter would be gone. Annette's sister lived in Montana and she had made arrangements to stay with her for awhile. Annette hadn't unpacked their clothes from the trip to the mountains so she threw what little belongings they were taking in the car, scribbled a quick note to Ben, and she and Hunter headed north. She didn't want to leave her husband but she had warned him what would happen if he brought Bethany home. He hadn't listened. She loved Ben dearly and maybe someday they could be together again but not as long as Bethany was in her home. Annette turned off her phone. She didn't want to talk to anyone right now.

Ben had been driving for about forty five minutes when he decided to call ahead to the hospital so Bethany could be ready to come home. The nurse on the other line seemed confused at his request. "Sir, Bethany left yesterday with her boyfriend. They said they were on their way to get married. I'm very sorry for the confusion but under state law she is an adult now." Ben was livid! He couldn't quite believe his ears. He immediately called his wife but with no answer. He turned his car around and headed home. "Well, Annette will be glad to hear this news," he thought, "but Bethany's life is ruined."

Bethany had left Bell a message on her answering machine telling her that she was getting married and she never wanted to see her mother again. Bell was devastated. She felt she had nothing left to live for. She knew what she would do. She rambled through her dresser drawers and found Ben's gun that she had hidden when they were married. It was still registered in his name. She made sure it was loaded and walked into her living room with her phone in hand. She had given this day a lot of thought. Ben was gone and now so was Bethany so she dialed 911.

"911 operator what is your emergency?"

"Help me! Help me!" Bell screamed into the phone, "My ex-husband has come into my house and is trying to kill me!" She knocked over a few items to make the call seem more believable. Then she screamed, "No! No! Please don't shoot!" Bell put the gun in her mouth and pulled the trigger. The sound was deafening as she fell to the floor. Her last conscious sound was the policemen kicking in her door. Bell lay in a puddle of blood and slipped into unconsciousness. Finally . . . Ben would pay for leaving her. The darkness engulfed her.